STARLIGHT: 150 POEMS

JOHN TRANTER is a leading contemporary English-language poet. He has published over twenty collections of verse and several anthologies and has given more than a hundred readings and talks around the world. He has visited New York City over twenty times, and has lived in London, Melbourne, Singapore, and elsewhere, and is now based in Sydney. He is the founding editor of the free internet magazine *Jacket* (*jacketmagazine. com*, 1997 to 2010, now *jacket2.org* at UPenn), the founder of the Australian Poetry Library project (*poetrylibrary.edu.au*) which publishes over 40,000 poems on the Internet, and the founder of the Journal of Poetics Research (*poeticsresearch.com*).

HIS HOMEPAGE at *johntranter.com* features over a thousand pages of poems, articles, reviews, interviews and critical material, including reviews of this book and extensive notes to many of the poems in it. More ephemeral items appear in his Journal (*johntranter.net*).

Also by John Tranter

Monographs:

Parallax
Red Movie
The Blast Area
The Alphabet Murders
Crying in Early Infancy: 100 Sonnets
Dazed in the Ladies Lounge
Selected Poems (1982)
Under Berlin
The Floor of Heaven
At The Florida
Gasoline Kisses
Different Hands (fiction)
Late Night Radio
Blackout
Ultra
Heart Print
The Floor of Heaven
Borrowed Voices
Studio Moon
Trio
Urban Myths: 210 poems: New and Selected
Ten Sonnets

Anthologies and compilations:

The New Australian Poetry
The Tin Wash Dish (poetry)
The Penguin Book of Modern Australian Poetry (co-editor)
Martin Johnston: Selected Poems and Prose

Starlight

150 Poems

John Tranter

BlazeVOX [books]
Buffalo, NY

Starlight: 150 Poems by John Tranter

Published by BlazeVOX [books]
Printed in the United States of America
This volume was first published by the University of Queensland
Press in 2010. All rights reserved. No part of this book may be
reproduced without the publisher's written permission, except for
brief quotations in reviews.

Book design by John Tranter and Geoffrey Gatza
Cover art: Louise Hearman: Untitled #1137, 2005
Oil on Masonite, 28 x 35cm. c/- Roslyn Oxley9 Gallery Pty Ltd,
Sydney, Australia.
Back cover photograph of John Tranter, Sydney, 2009,
by Anders Hallengren.

First American Edition
ISBN: 978-1-60964-165-8
Library of Congress Control Number: 2013953020

BlazeVOX [books]
131 Euclid Ave Kenmore, NY 14217
Editor@blazevox.org

publisher of weird little books

BlazeVOX [books]

blazevox.org

IT SEEMS NATURAL, in retrospect, that the first great surrealist poetry in English was written by an Australian, Ern Malley. The fact that he was a hoax hardly matters. The poetry is what does, and it's superb. It seems like modernism was directed at Australia like arrows from all over the world, and gets shot back in tenfold multiplications of them. Certainly John Tranter, who has been an international phenomenon for some time, is not one to deny the influences from outside, or to slow down the discussion of whether it all (Beats, Black Mountain, New York School) may be a hoax itself. This open question is, after all, what gives them their plangency and liveliness. We can find here firmly planted echoes of O'Hara — ('The Last Clean Shirt') with its superb first line, 'We have to make do with Third Avenue,' Ashbery — 'The Anaglyph,' Charles Baudelaire — 'The Age of Nakedness,' with its lovely ending, 'A way of being astonished / by little things: a tractor, a running fox, a harbour full of boats,' and no doubt others as well, but Tranter's genius is singular in both senses of the word. Does he contain multitudes? Yes, he contains multitudes. His version of 'Lights on the Hill' assembles an odd bunch of artists: Stanley Spencer, Fantin-Latour, Bacon, Rockwell, Picasso, Pollock, Whiteley (don't know him) and Warhol, and concludes 'These curses, these futile blasphemies, these / hangovers, larger than the Brooklyn Bridge, / sobs, headaches, hissy fits, pissing competitions, / they are a kind of veterinary vitamin injection, / fit to raise a snoring draught-horse to his duties...' Welcome to Tranter's medicinal coruscating world. You'll like it. It'll do you good.

– John Ashbery

Acknowledgment is due to the editors of the magazines in which some of the poems in this volume first appeared: *Age* (Melbourne, Australia), *Antipodes*, *Argotist* (online), *Australian*, *The Best Australian Poems* 2010 (R. Adamson, Ed.), *Blackbox Manifold* (online), *Connotation Press: An Online Artifact*, *Fulcrum* (Boston, USA), *Jacket* magazine (online), *Masthead* (online), *The Modern Review* (Toronto), *Southerly* magazine.

For J.A.

'... time for coffee and a Strega at *Il Miglior Fabbro*.'

Contents

Three Poems

The Anaglyph

Hasn't the charisma leaked away from the café crowd, and that other
Authority, the *Salon des Refusés*? I have forgotten much of
That old sack of enthusiasms and snake-oil recipes, the way
You have forgotten your own childhood, since
You woke up just in time to watch the adults disappear
From the world they had bequeathed us. It seems the scenery all around
Is hilly and unfarmable. Being brilliant has been reckoned
Into a procedure by some old guy, with a motto that is
More fitness, less flab. I hanker to go back to the land.
This means ruin to the culture-watchers. But the basic
Principle of my ambition is to be one excessively distracted
Entity at the mercy of the lurid, blurred and half-perceived
Motions of the Martians at the Halloween Hop. Fake? They sure are.
Summer is called Humidor here, the month of damp draughts.
The tale of my attempt to farm stubborn soil leaked from
Untruth to legend, my unlikely phase of boy-scout honesty being
Before I came to the big city. Here behind the tiny horological waterfall
Drums amplify the fun, but only at nightfall, then just for a moment
Of horrible error as I clutch the wrong person's hand. That was true,
Only I said it wrong. Ugh. Now watch my serpentine
Gesture as I withdraw my hand, only to replace it with a congruent
Message that attempts to excuse this tactless fact,
Tearing at the sky over Twenty-second Street, but
The sky leans nonchalantly against the coop – I mean 'co-op' – about
As graceful as a cowboy leaning on a chicken co-op – I mean 'coop' –
                                        who either
Has an anger management problem or is under the influence of a form of
Some anxiety that eats at him. I'm not the fly-away
Marrying kind, nor a grumpy bachelor with a broken heart whose pieces
Are seen scattered over the range. That begs for an independent
Yet symbolic judgment from the Judge now alighting from the caboose,
                                        whose arrival
Whether timely, to the tick of a caesium atom, or tardy, has to be
Seen to be believed, like
The face of a hunter in the dim mirror killing a bear. As
Nostrils give away suppressed anger by flaring, so an argument
That is over leaves traces – nervous twitch, grimace. It

Is impossible to hide my feelings, I guess. Look ahead,
That effervescent persona and its emotional lurches and rocketings
Affected so much, and its magnum opus that was called
By another name is now the old school-teacher's chief creed and belief,
Or something very like it, gleaming in the rain. Hold up that light.
Has it shone on the tenebrous backyards yet? Or yet admitted that
It is unable to illuminate the wasteland of wet barbecues, so much
Of its fuel has flared and lit up the landscape... this project, I admit that
It is like gutting then refurbishing a friend's apartment. Now, are
The reply and the echo done with? I asked a redundant question, and
That answer suffocated it, as a firmly pressed pillow
Has choked a banker, but no one knows whodunnit. That whole thing
Of returning to my sources, raking through my prototypes until
The last blueprint is found and seems just right: perhaps this is
Peace – a crowded peace – under the hot sun.
That we are afraid of it – inhabiting a reputation, the whole thing
About establishing who you genuinely were – are – I'll admit. There
You hope your opus will be taken for legerdemain, but your effort sinks
Deeper into the mulch of history, while I adjust the mask that
Just fits more loosely every decade, and then I add up the little
That memory leaves me, a kind of pittance, the totality
Mustered and gathered... a look of boredom in a young person's eyes,
And all those hopes and struggles are quite lost.
Accents and dialects distort them, once again.
To have escaped from a tangle of difficulties, from
Nothing but obstructions, into a glowing absence
And then to take a deep breath and plunge into
Those crowded riverine cities, greedy for contact with ghosts that are
Precisely what we want them to be, our plans furthered,
Seeing alphabet soup spell out the aleatory message and the time,
Casting caution to the winds and the weather – sorry, welter
Of neighbours, barking dogs, traffic cops in a dreadful confusion.
And permit me... no, commit me, please, while the cops are standing
Around chewing the fat, and pray that these
Moments miss you like a whistling arrow. Thunk! The old tapir tapered
Into the bar: a Scotsman, an Italian, and a capybara – I've heard it. But
Wasn't the story of an Eskimo inside an eviscerated bear like this?
The fact that he 'inhabited' the smelly bear-skin... I feel that
Neither brave feats nor stories about them can cut it.

Did not a Dandy Dinmont yap? I deliberately stayed
This way, spiritually a hunchback, drooling and gaping at the stars
That promised ashes and diamonds and nourishing food all the way,
As though clambering inside an animal was simply the reverse
Of some method of becoming notorious. My cheating heart is known
Once its modus operandi is – among the cognoscenti – firmly established.
The look of a man is the man, Buffon said, and style a condition
Of those whose reputation is a handbag and whose blindness
Was being talked about even in Paris: a troubling myopia, so
That their left and right perceptual fields, red and green, slowly separated,
Only to hitch up again, like inspiration and perspiration. Go on, shout
And be heard. Is this anaglyph what I really want? My declamatory
Nature was made to seem just a yokel act. I must admit it is
Not without a certain eau-de-cologne charm, insinuated the farmer. And yet
An invisible dread prevents me making love to you among the previsions,
Then the post-visions that afflict me arrive, fits of
The assurance Baron Corvo had an excess of, a crowing assurance
Which tainted his career, under the blasts of air conditioning,
Whatever. There on the bank statement
At the beginning of the Age of Façadism was a catalogue of waste.
A dumb waiter brought me the tablets and a note about the projected
After-effects: they may amplify the symptoms instead of curing them,
Though Frederick Rolfe was never cured. This
Emptiness will do fine. Just pop it in a doggy bag, thanks. Did you
                                        say 'previsions'?
Was that a mispronunciation? 'Provisions', maybe, held
Too close to the chest, a fake poker hand of fate. The fireworks, they
Ended with a fizzing Roman candle sound that frightened the guest who was
Intended to rescue Gertie McDowell from that dirty old man. It's
Gesture that fills out the role, as water makes the weather.
It was stupid of me to harp on the sadness
Of that animal's demise: I should forget about the feeling
Which resembles taxidermy at midnight on an empty highway.
A telescope brings us a soothing view of distant mountains
And all the mountain people. Who knows where they're going?
Moving from crag to cave to avoid the night
There, which is really ghastly when it comes on.
Beside the darkness, each farmer carries his own personal
Landscape around inside his head, a 'landscape' being

What surrounds your idea of yourself, it's so
Honourably framed, but presented in a Potemkin-village spirit.
There was a vast electrical disturbance just outside the walls.
Each time it's different, down through the centuries
For the sake of cultural improvements they repeat a dream that
Continually gives out a soft fluorescent glow, it was
Like standing on the prow of a moving ferry in the morning
With the spray bursting all around
And a feeling of nausea mixed with ecstasy washing over me. In a way
The whole experience was fake, except for the scale.
Really, what do Eskimos think of giants?
Not too much, I reckon. They say they like them.
A moment later they're saying how needlessly big they are. But
Also they are likely to flatter them. A cloud of dust
Or whirling fragments resembling a mistral rises up ahead,
But no one understands it: the old verbal torrent
In new guise, transformed into a sheaf of falling leaves, which
Are gathered up, bound, and stuffed into a briefcase,
And it's time for coffee and a Strega at *Il Miglior Fabbro*. When
Acts of killing fill nightmares and movies, only the calm
Of this bibulous routine can bring surcease. Then the shreds
Of another adventure assemble: a tour of the old college premises
Undertaken to the tune of the jig 'From Rochester he came hence,
A writ of Cease and Desist clenched in his teeth'. Here, see this,
Like a pistol on a silver platter, it's all yours
And it was mine once. Take it, go on. I kept it because
It had been handed down, and I had hoped it might be my insurance
Against the waves of devoted fans incfficiently
Seeking to take over the social scene and then the whole world.
The round platter, alas, has always been covered with dust,
So small it can hardly hold the pearl-handled revolver reclining on it.
Thereafter it should be passed on to other worthies, noted by
The comfort of strangers they fail to offer you, or me, even.
Like the wily coyote, I'm no sleep-abed; I tried all
The most difficult forms, even threnodies ending with the words
'After all' or 'Never mind!' And in my fine eye-rolling frenzy I almost
Exaggerated my métier into an obligation. This,
It seemed, was the way to build the future. But it was
Not likely to allow me to escape the whirligig of voracious time.

After all, *tempus fugit*, however we might chase it. Indeed,
All kinds of regret sprinkled my breakfast as the slant angle of
The day lit up the diner and the light began to increase
So that I was dazzled, then I heard a loud thump, dull, heavy,
Like a polar bear falling over, and the hunter saying something
Not quite obscene, but close enough. *Criminy!* The way
Things fade away, *le temps perdu* seems to be the point
Of this rodomontade. Does a traditional verse form simply provide
A protected place for the poet to plead the case for his vital
Concern for *la vie littéraire*, or is it a carapace, a palace?
And you can meditate there all summer long.
It was a little insight I had, one of the world's smallest.
Distant requests annoy me. The Poetry Club may be ultra-sensitive
But its supine and self-serving acquiescence
To the demands of those creeps... okay, that's in the past
And it belongs there and I promised not to whine. But oh, how
The past haunts me, its vapid fashions, the rigmaroles... they wish
But also harangue, that's why I resent them, the ones I talk with.
And in this way my paean to non-discovery
In brittle yet oracular verse persuades us, but nevertheless
The map you provided was helpful in leading us beyond
Madness to something better: squatting in Circe's mansion. Only
You desire us to fail – just there, perhaps, where your verbal acts
Are sentinels warning us of the slow-moving, quiet
Invasion of middle America by pod people over many years.
Be quiet – hush! – they are nearby, whispering the poem itself
In a parody of oratory. I'll explain more plainly: the map
Of the literary world is a pantomime, and its longueurs have become
Prolongations of our prevarications on bad weather days, and also
Fine days where things seem okay but are not, those dull events
We shall banish from the Ideal Republic. Who called? No, I am
Not speaking to that shit: he just wants to be
Opposite me at the literary lunch. He got some fame recently, only
To be thrust into obscurity soon, I hope. It seems broader,
The sum total, a canal reflecting its own anagram, but will it ever
Become legible? Hidden behind a screen of rocks
And foliage, the creep quickly inhales the distant
Ether and faints, thank goodness, and what I own
I see before me shining like a dagger. Meanwhile

I am only me, a faithful shadow of my real self, and
Private doubts evaporate between the Spring and the Fall
And even this is seasonal, and I thank you
For being so patient, you could have made some other
Voluntary or involuntary gesture like sneezing to prove your
Maturity or you could have hung and dangled from the branches
Of a tree to attract my attention a step or two away from them.
It intensifies my desire to know you, a gesture like that, to
Form an opinion of your feints, apparitions and mode of locomotion.
In this way I control the crowded avenue to the Palace of Fame, the one
Leading to a rowboat mounted in a park where I perch and think to
Myself and then jot it down, being careful to leave a blank space
That is the secret indication of Mallarmé's abyss, a.k.a. 'The Unknown.'
Eating ragwort is morally better than gobbling a quail tagine; the difference
Can never be explained to the obtuse. At this distance
It seemed impossible to reach the reader, Valéry murmured, then said
                                        the phrase
'Over and over' to himself, again and again. Meanwhile
Infant mortality was declining as aspirin consumption increased. There was
To be a meeting about aspirin and other drugs later that evening,
He was told. He read poems about killing large animals to keep awake
On the tepid waters of café society. Go to the meeting, don't go, whatever.
'Whose centre wobbles must fail,' the Latin motto says, and having
The progression of the equinox too much in mind brings rain
As they form a phalanx of epigones, those who come after.
Why don't they just get used to that? They can't be equal
Without coming before, and that's impossible. The cup of
Contentment will never touch their lips. Ministering
To stunted talents is my fate; each day I tread that lonesome trail alone
And return at nightfall bereft and grinding my teeth at
What they dish out: similes as appliqué aperçus. They
Might as well hand in embroidery. The Force, puissant yet invisible,
Still surrounds us. Yet there is also a Dark Force
Between the cruel mandates of history and them.
It is because the greatness of art is like a snobbish relative
That we shall never agree on a strategy, and
Entertainment washes over us, leaving us ethically incomplete.
Former East German border guards know too well that that
Closes off an awful lot of options. The Moment

Of Death is dallying on Ninth Avenue, as yet uncertain of
Its intentions. I'll just leaf through the paper until
You wake up. I'm not planning to go anywhere. You know, it
Wasn't a small thing, to turn your back on Europe. The walls
Are turning into their own murals. Please don't speak
Of time within the hearing of that tiny hydraulic clock you
Invented, it can be self-centred and jealous, and has now
Grown furious. Deep within its complex innards a purple jewel
Exists as a blazon, rotating slowly, saying that this
Existence is temporary, that you may lodge and idle here
Only so long as you don't irritate the gods. Someone's
Purpose niggles at you. Then the sunbeams flood in at acute
Angles and frighten the other diners. I thought, then,
Of having whatever I wanted, but it seemed that a distant
Image of you chided me. My admiration is a test
Of how you might accept it: gracefully, or boorishly, or not.
You hesitate, don't you? I hate that. Please accept this
Wooden gesture, and you're right, the over-decorated representation
Returns whence it came, though it was easily said, and simply meant,
With nothing ulterior about it: a *simple entendre*. I'd like to alight
With you from the caboose on a hot dry day in a wonderful town. You
Must help the Judge measure the exact length of the shadow of
Your well-wrought urn in the centre of the square – it is still intact;
Appreciation gives it the shine and the shadow – but just now somebody
Is phoning to arrange for drinks – will you join me? – later this evening.

Desmond's Coupé

Desmond's coupé is full of jam. He's in a quandary:
a bean lance, or a dance of circumstances.
He's eternally fond of his own naivety.
A swanky beam spells out a white
cranky tale.

Susan's inclination was
plainly desperate.

An ailment common in Sienna
makes him think he's dead and buried
or makes him realise he's a bad dresser
on a plane, or in jail, but you don't dress for jail
and people don't wear a jacket on a plane any more.
Raise the bonds.

His three résumés – swallowed – he's just
a shadow of his former self – phooey! – a deep violet colour,
or an alternative he'll just have to adapt to
by the verge of the road.

Deep beans: his aunt has a rooster.
She's getting battier every year,
a fish in one hand, a peach in the other.

The Master of Surges,
or so we infer.

In the flames we see the communist menace –
uniquely, they've got the numbers, no?
But they hesitate when the corpse waves its arms.
Pluto (not Mickey) wants to play,
oh, what a nut! Chained
at the party, a name for the horse floats,
an old horse works it out,
tapping his hoof on the floor, good trick,
but then forgetting how old he is
behind the jade barrier.

#

These pedals take you to an agreeable horizon,
well prepared.

You old git, free meals,
a bad smell on the dratted train –
now he's heading for the air vents
in another carriage –
that's the spirit – actually, a jet plane
would be quite a temptation.
You could re-employ a division of passing firemen.

The secret item on the menu,
the chef's envy, even now
is cooling on the barbecue, or so you surmise.

Look straight at the homosexual:
nerveless, not very important, yet vain,
an old Hoover in his hand.

Potato crisps
are found in the deli, useless for a téte-â-tète.

He takes a disprin and feels legless, then he
has another one, then he feels
ambiguous. His ulterior plans
are unforgettably demonic.
He feels nothing
for the empty countries, Alaska, let's say,
home of the Inuit. This old idiot
had a chance to meet The Supremes, probably –
say, Louie, your son is some puerile *hombre*,
caressing a policeman and renting out a lavatory,
eating soup and getting vaguer –
a soup full of hard bones,
now he enters the aisle, bending his knee
like a bat flapping into the sea.
The old tenant reads Lowell ['s poem] against the sea,
a chance to ooze poetry –
financially speaking, that is – no, don't –

a voile handkerchief is an illusion
as antsy as having a phantom for a guest
in the chancellery
but that won't abolish folly
like this insinuating silence
or Dan's squelchy high-voltage approach –
he's simply rolling around and laughing ironically.
Ooo! – A mystery!
A precipice!
Frank Hurley!
A billion turbots! Laughter and horror
with the author Jimmy Giuffre (tenor sax),
but no junkies, please,
no fur,
and that old berk verging on the index
like so, a lonely puff of smoke at Purdue –
so far, so good,

where recounting the effluent is the talk of the minute,
and it immobilises you.

A chiffon and velour coffee-coloured sombrero
for this stiff old white man
is derisory, an opposition horse seal,
rather tropical, the sombrero, quite unmarked,
exhumed, quite conkers,
the American prince who loves the cool,
he gives a little heroic cough.

Irresistible maize container!

Par for the course, but a pretty feeble reason to be acting virile
and like a foodie, maybe the ulcers explain his puberty
or mute his loose and bossy vinaigrette
(invisible from the front)
sparkling with umbrage,
with the stature of a shadowy filet mignon
and with the torsion of a siren
impatient at squeamish ultimatums.
A rare, yes, and vertiginous debut.

Time to snaffle
a bifurcated soufflé,
thinks the old bird.

His manner is rather false.
All up, with a toilet next to the bedroom,
evaporated brooms
impose an unborn infinite state
issuing from the stars – *que sera, sera* –
a pyre doesn't disadvantage the minors,
they're indifferent to the mutants,
that is, to the number of mutants that exist
apart from those agonising, sparse
hallucinations of mutants which start when they stop
and never seem to close, apparently, with an infant.

The park elk and his profusion of expandable rarities –
see, then the chief rat is ill –

evidence that the Battle of the Somme, for one of us at least
was a poor thing, though somehow illuminating
and written up in Hansard.

Choose a pen.

A left-hand drive car with a rhythmic suspension
that levels itself, an ox and some original scum,
no more wars, a delirious sound and just one crime
fleeing without identifying Jimmy Giuffre's true neutrality.

Rein in a memorable crisis
as you see fit.
Your venomous accomplice can view the results: nothing!
Nothing human, that is.

In lieu of an aura of elevation,
the absence of ordinary verse.

In the loo, an inferior kind of clap
is likely to disperse and conquer

those who act in a poor video.
Abruptly key the synonym.

Parson, men's songs are fond of perdition.

A dance, in the garage full of vague parables,
and which reality is dissolved?
Except where the altitude peters out
and an Aussie's loins are right on.

A few swans, a vector dealer and
a horse of interest –
and a quantity of signals in general sell on,
tell obliquities, part Elle's declivities –
the furs, poems, see what theatre
a septuagenarian from the far north of Australia
sees in the stars – freezing, oblique and full of suet –
pass the aunt –
a killer from Noumea –
and this vacant surface is superior
to any successive hurt.

Side-rail was meant –
done, counted, totalled information
and a veiled ant, doubts, the rolls...

brilliantly meditating before the ratter
whose pointed bum is sacred –
and all the pensioners met Des and his coupé.

Five Quartets

1

All might have been speculation.
What might have been opened?
I do not inhabit the garden.
There they were dignified, invisible,
over the dead bird, in response to

the flowers that are our guests,
in the drained pool.
Dry water, bird children,
garlic and mud in the blood
dance along the sodden floor.
Below, the practical *Erhebung* without
elimination, its partial ecstasy,
its horror. Yet the body cannot
allow a little dim light: strained fancies
with no men. Bits of wind in unwholesome
eructation, the torpid gloomy hills of Putney,
twittering into inoperancy and the other.
Abstention from its metalled bell
carries the cling wing.

2

Words move the Chinese violin, while
words between the foliage
waste a factory, or a by-pass.

There is a time for the wind to break
and to shake the field-mouse with a silent motto.

You lean against a van
and the deep village, the sultry dahlias,
wait for the early pipe.

3

And the little man and woman
round and round the fire
leaping through the laughter
lifting the milking and the coupling
of man and woman of dung and wrinkles.
I am here in heat, and writhing high
into grey roses filled with thunder.
The rolling cars weep and hunt the ice.
That was not very worn-out.
Poetical fashion, wrestle with poetry.
Calm and wisdom deceived us, the dead secrets
into which they turned their every moment,
and shocking monsters, fancy old men,
can hope to acquire houses under the Stock Exchange.

4

The Directory of cold lost the funeral.
I said to the dark, the lights are hollow,
with a bold rolled train in the Tube
and the conversation fades into the mental ether,
the mind is in the garden, pointing and repeating
'there is no ecstasy!' The wounded steel,
the fever chart, is the disease,
the dying nurse our hospital.
The millionaire ascends from feet to mental wires.
I must quake in our only drink, blood.

#

Trying to use a failure, because one has
shabby equipment in the mess of emotion,
and to conquer men, is no competition.
Home is older, stranger, intense.
But the old lamplight is nearly here,
with the explorers.

5

I think that the patient is forgotten.
Men choose the machine, but the nursery bedroom
in the winter gaslight is within us,
also the algae and the dead men.
The sea has the water,
the groaner and the women.

Where is there an end of it?

Where is the end of the wastage?
We have to think of them,
while the money is ineffable:

we appreciate the agony of others,
covered by dead negroes.

Speaking French

Hôtel de Ville

The kids should visit a history museum
in their senior year, to understand disgrace as
one form of Clinton's victory. On the other hand
the European Community foreign debt gives
everybody bad dreams. So we do need to solve
the problem of students reading difficult things
that will lead them astray: why did Rimbaud
turn from socialism to capitalism? As if
it matters. He is his own consolation prize.
We'd be delighted to have his uniform.
We want to see all the modern art stuff, too.
Thank you. Press the button marked 'monument'
and see what happens: a recorded voice says
'I have wasted my life', and we pay to listen.

Deluge

Upgrading the late edition for all US units.
So why didn't you clear the town square?
In the thievery of my own dreams I can see
the square like a crystal showing a blurry
and refracted image of twenty people protesting.
Sure, you visited downtown Los Angeles:
it was always November there. You do not get that
on the Internet. The patrol has no qualms about
going on, and later we delivered the women
to encourage the men to start moving and get
that problem solved – it became the key
that unlocked the pain of the Soviet Union, and
today there's a new location for the war movie,
a green meadow filled with buttercups.

Ornery

We did want to buy the Kennedy memento.
The sun is rising and you'll get the crop,
but you are the harvest and not the reaper.
The light shone on the barn, full of wheat.
Who are those guys, in suits, with guns?
The CIA. One is a dish of blood. The other:
stains on the carpet, red tadpoles lisping.
They put the guns away, and listen.
It is off the hook, the phone. Their clothing
failed to blend with the rural scenery. Now
the agents call – 17 men – that is safe to assume –
and claim that the assassination never happened.
There was no song the Nashville people liked
in that field of political and human damage.

Democracy

Well, there goes compulsory voting: the Americans
want to keep the freedom to be governed by
corrupt politicians elected by somebody else.
So much for the tools of democracy.
Talk to the PC makers. We need cheaper
entertainment, not cheaper political displays.
They use our money to promote themselves
so they can take our money again.
To see it all, but to miss that one second
when the gun is fired... there's an old saying:
How much water is needed to run a horse?
I'd be interested in hearing your reply.
Today your wanderings have come full circle,
and you will tell us everything you know.

Royalties

We'll make common cause with the Right,
and take that message to the Ford Foundation
who helped the CIA guy in Paris win a medal
that let him sit in on the cultural deliberations
of all those old freaks, whose virtue is really
stubbornness. The quote of the week missed me –
that is, I missed it – I just stopped by
to look in on the literary debate, cast a vote…
Democracy is what we define it to be.
Sure the Iranians voted in a government,
but those socialist shits were going to nationalise –
their oil, British oil, our oil, what the hell –
so we put in that poet guy to agitate, Bunting.
Sure, people were killed: so what?

Pronto

No joy in this one, Bob. Would you like to be
summoned for a little blot on the record,
by a marshal, you who were always in the way?
And list the indictment today, that will be
implemented tomorrow? If you do that, old friend,
the problem seems to be saying, the data
will go on the skids – it could be a fun contest
held in a field in the Boston area.
Now I don't want you to get the idea that
finding a guitar has anything to do with it.
Just dish it up like the boss wants: though
if you deal with the CIA – Hi – I'm Bob.
Can't talk now. Down in the park,
listening to the guitars, lots of single mothers…

Departure

In this view
of *La Comédie Humaine*
we see only postures
of the dream, and this one
becomes a nightmare
when you turn on the light
and listen to the news
on the pound and the dollar
or the euro
on a fix –
so much for
the public
who know it
in the wallet.

The Fixer

Call me. The distant box is open. It has
the fix-it, though in three days of using it
he just couldn't get through to the end
of 'log enable'. You have to pay for that stuff.
He had a stiff drink or two in a cool bar
then the investigating court claimed
that the CIA under any other name
would be the same people: incompetents.
The defendants are free to come and go
as they please, through the vanilla-flavoured
venetian blinds. Incompetent killers, I mean,
but someone has to do it, I guess. This idea
is not the only derivative thing to happen
in the tasteful colonial novel of manners.

Metro

Two guys from Detroit pored over the suicide letter
as its auction price rose through the $8.oo range.
A male choir that this year sang in Vietnam
is now a medical team on a training course.
No one wants an incontinent hostage.
Mother's call for us all to share the pretty things
fell on deaf ears; so much for the taste of justice.
They can't be bought. An investigation will not
reveal me as a donor or a smaller companion.
The promise of learning is a delusion. That's what
befalls most of us plagiarists: our suckers
reject the disillusion that comes with the ugly truth.
One guy says the people in the movie are people;
but I say no one is a real actor in the film.

Movements

The guys in the Gulf of Aden did enough,
but the President said to kill one of those bad
men on Friday, bring the body to him later.
To call the team 'failures' would make this
a political stumble. The girls are young
and silly: Girls, your heads are full of boys,
why, in the hot flush of adolescence –
of all the kids in this town, why should you –
yet if I want to take you on my lap and act romantic
it's No Way, José. If you go from the beach to
the Hotel for the Young and the Stupid, you'll see
that we don't need more expensive scriptwriters,
just a few idiots to improvise dialogue. Just
blabber: that sounds fine and energetic.

Flowers

Jim Gott and old money don't mix. There is
no possibility of change. He sent flowers
to the old lady, to no avail. Then he fought
the Chinese laundry over the disputed crease
in his last clean shirt sent by UPS; the Chinaman
got a court order that he not be so called.
He makes peanuts: Jim's thousand a year is viewed
as a decent living: you figure it out.
Old Gott was taken to court, a kind of
maze synod, that September, ornamental
cherry petals littering the streets.
Thirty-eight years later the charge sheet tells us
that he was called The Fiendish. In the distant
future, I shall be as efficient as you.

Horticulture

Thomas Cecil, what did you do?
The autobiography will have to be cancelled.
Thomas was sued by the city
because he gave a false statement
when he came to the desert resort
with a female companion, named 'The Wife'.
A man can get what he wants on the inside –
but that didn't do Old Tom much good.
Thomas abducted the lady, but then he said
in fact he was giving her the holiday she needed,
and wanted, had she only known it, and
getting her to admit it to herself, well,
that was the problem for Old Thomas, and now
he has time on his hands, and may yet solve it.

Anguish

The May frostbite is still on the land,
a statement by analogy
down by John Quinn.
We should assess this.
Single men sit through the night,
nursing a grudge and a stiff whisky,
and a beaker of wine
darker than the deepest twilight.
Flying, all share a common fear.
My initials in the sky. She's clinging to
the grab handle, waiting for the lurch.
Why did I ask her along? Oh, sure,
thanks for joining in the song, as the plane
lands in the Land of the Closet Morons.

Barbarians

In the state-house today old McAfee
told his story, and none too soon. It is cool
and dim inside, but the patio is sunny.
He is only local news in a local court, but
I was worried. What if he cracked? The media
were there, barbaric on the video phones.
They're seeing it like so: he has a free kick.
Did you say 'What happened to the eighties?'
Are they the only ones saying this lady
made a few dents in the system,
took her doses – I see it as two doses –
and then a plea bargain for the shopping assault?
This edition paints it as a gamble on love, or a kiss
too soon, or Mondo music and a new full moon.

Bottom of the Harbour

Maria today got a heap of stuff,
all she can use for a month.
Taylor said she should take one
for the Indian, that is, the male person
originally from the subcontinent
and since she wasn't being the buyer
for two of them, she said no. There was
calm rapture in the way she spoke.
This had an effect on the warrior courtroom.
Do you mean that the US should give up
the Cold War tactics shown on the
Canton blankets? We use them to keep warm,
for goodness' sake, it's a case of being up at dawn
bottom-feeding in and around the drowned cathedral.

Dawn

The judge will get a jury together, don't worry:
the system was breaking down, but a fix is just
a phone call away. Then they can open the case.
There are more witnesses to be called, so
keep an eye on what he wants. Really,
all these criminals and junkies are the envy
of a bevy of affected socialites. That is,
their manners are affected, not their health.
The studies say the middle classes need a hit
of guilt, once a week. Don't ask me why. For them
the 'don't feel safe' area reads 'black and Latino'
area. Something about rebels white-anting
the floor they're standing on: a turn-on.
On Monday a lesson on the genesis of Genesis.

Parade

The beautiful city is his only speaking song,
a song that took place in the open air,
and we also collected data based on a dream,
the presumed landscape and the dream of home.
It's a CD of Fall songs, maybe, only
the data is in a format that might give away
the occupation of the person, and as we clambered
into the shuttle, a flashlight shone on the ticket.
So the district judge knows that I am still at large,
thanks to the informers the courts imprisoned.
They added a goal to motivate the contestants
and that's one of the ideas they need to speed up:
the one who collects forgotten languages will be sad:
the words of all the songs have been forgotten.

Scenes From a Voyage

The passengers are delirious, staring at the sea.
The slide presentation featured the Deutsche Bahn AG
then the attendees took off their clothes... the news
spread like wildfire through the luxury liner –
Ronald, stop them! Don't shout! Or give orders!
We told the passenger what the passenger wants.
We've only potted palms, and one wolf a year.
Then all the comedians disembark in San Diego.
That's a tour plan with a real future, though
the Torture Room is daunting, I agree,
and I should say that the ticket sale failed
because of that. They even want to set up
cameras in the bedrooms. We'll all need visas,
for this is the land where hope turns to fear.

Sorehead

I was arrested because of that internal memo,
and ended up in a cell, then I was told to sit
with the police and the local bigwigs.
In the hushed and fast darkening room they said
someone – *someone* – had reduced the safety margin
on the airport risk factor, and I got the blame.
The sky that day was a pale, clear blue, but
that was happening outside, and far away.
The cop on duty would not open the tomb
of the deported – sorry, departed – and as usual
he had a story. Every movie, he said, depends
on a script, and the narrative grows out of
market research: a set of standard deviations. Art?
What would they know? Open the tomb, and let me in.

Eighteen Fairies

Eighteen sequential disasters this year,
that's what happens when you plant the seed
and don't plan how to reap the crop.
One symphony after another, concert
after concert, and the audiences howling
for entertainment, but all they got was anguish.
He had great reviews, from his pals, but that was
backwash from the counter-culture of the sixties.
I am up to date, he said. Was that immodest?
Well, fuck you. He had the reputation, not the talent,
traffic increasing on the freeway, and somehow
with his life written out in waves of music,
he knew he was a saint, but the sainthood, alas,
was as a false light to all the roaring day.

The New Music

Its stated goal is an assault on the old music.
The norm for most jazz pianists: a jug
of kitsch filled with noises, cocktail chatter.
But she is the editor of a different algorithm,
turning out waves of music that feed me several
emotions, that avoid the tradition of discourse
and last longer than their own recordings.
That's why I quit and took up writing poetry
instead. But I guess that was a mistake.
Are the blues just a warp in the DNA,
a genetic splice on the silver bullet of jazz?
At the beginning of the major slowdown
music is used to liven up the dismal matter
late at night when every gesture is cool.

Genius

Diary jotting: be innovative, nouveau. Hey,
that was an ad that makes use of its own
matching channel as a greed altar, but
hungers are just another topic, to them,
and a decent cost analysis is still needed.
The BBC wanted to see if that moment still has
a null market, or can they kick it into life?
They only sell movies they don't have the ending for.
For that large a show, get a couple to fight
a ban made up of forcible sodomy law.
'Separated at birth' is all the formatting you need.
You know where: what tools to use, you know
what to say: we diva the couple to do a little more,
and as for shared data, forget it: see 'soufflés, social'.

Lives

Put me on the list of local media maniacs.
I am an old man working on a dBase file,
barely tolerated, living on the margin,
and I know that all the men in the city
are there for a reason. And then the insane visual
was invented, the Enola come-on. Come on,
I can't hear you. Take the kids to see the conditions
caused by the Vietnam War, why don't you?
They're not humane in Dawson City.
It seems to me that your famous design champion
is up a tree, and what effect does that have
on the practical Mister? Mama must do
what she must, shut down by the town marshal
as a mandate for the people of Mormon.

Martian Movie

What to do? Just wake up to see if the units
wake up. Keep this idea like a jet in a hangar.
You might be the key that all three of us need –
(and Jimmy the Basin) – need to be on call to notify
Kitty and the target – oh the arduous trade –
do the scene – of what, may I ask? – the scene
where some guy keeps keying the Martian
into frame. How? I don't know. I'm a writer,
and all we know is how to create the creature,
not its morals. Our ambition: to be small and clear
and free. I'm resting now in the slough where Rocco
and his brothers take over the joint. The navy is in town
and that guy called Austin is struggling to decode
the signals. Yet the tomb riddle will be solved.

New Beauty

Being viewed as both coward and hero
is debilitating; night after night this message
returns, soaking into your dreams, and
naturally you try to deceive the onlookers,
and then you want to sound as though you are
playing with a famous band, creating huge
drafts of music that rush through the city
that may be Sydney, and then again it may not.
So you pour all your resources into the battle
to get to the top of the pops with your angry music,
and force the listeners around the Pacific rim
to vote your way: most are no friends of America.
The airplane to you is that person, a star,
rising high and then falling. That's the Catch 22.

Dolls

Being viewed as a combination of beauty and ugliness
is a debilitating affliction: with a false face
and a different coat you would try to deceive them:
out of the dreamwork of night the token emerges
in the music store, and they want to sound like
something that's already popular and thus
almost out of date. Fashion has to change:
that's its essence. One day enduring values reign,
then around the Pacific rim, Structured Query Language
is pestering the database for more and better data.
Then again, you may get sacked; then where's your
cocky prognostication? Knee-deep in bullshit, a failure
relayed over the Captain's headset on final approach:
and the country you land in is not America.

Childhood

Combing your hair, you think you look great, but
you look all blotchy on the late show, performing
for thousands of people, and indeed the team
in the studio including John Updike and a close
female friend cast doubt on the audience figures.
Then a movie set in Vietnam, young guys
dying in a fire-fight, but on a neighbouring island
the locals benefit from new lease of life.
The audience absorbs the pain, and each time
the movie repeats they become more inured
to the sight of their tax dollars being showered
among the executives employed by the military-
industrial complex, and used to kill foreigners.
This movie schedule is layered and glowing.

Brooklyn

Less program, more ads, that's what
the people want, they need a piss break
every hour. Rewind: a bang on the gong
and he's off to Brooklyn, sun blinding him,
he has the votes to win the best slot of the night,
baseball game cancelled, trouble breathing,
cost of sales ballooning – this is the
'FM in a Domain Name System' hazard,
a collapse they share with the boss who demands
we solve it – what the consumers want –
extra pay, he would say that to keep me,
but I'm used to his lies. Sufficient
unto the day are its many small evils –
Betty, comment on that, pronto.

Shames

Don't kid me, I'm not Noah. The corps
existed in the new data – esprit
de corps, I mean – I mean give-away,
no way – people see the wheel
then get a phenomenal fright. No one
thought she did it – she and the Nazi,
baking bread in a cosy home in the Midwest.
Men appear, but they live in boxes.
Call me 'wish of the mall' and no,
I don't want the Tutsi player.
Make a decision on the whole movie:
good or bad. Mary is no relation.
Kitty cat, you force the Nazi salute.
I need what? A system of stone?

Story

The police tracked them to a cheap motel
on the edge of town, bugged the joint,
got a heap of so-called evidence: it seems
they're holding a playboy, he is on the sofa,
unconscious, unable to consider the eulogy
the papers were quick to publish, fairly rich
but hardly an intellectual, in plain fact
thick as a brick, but as I say, loaded.
Today a new approach: baby the thugs
and hope to sneak in under their radar,
play soothing music at deafening levels,
knock them out with logical conundrums.
Doctor Plausible gets the nod. In the scene
that no one wants you to see, they all get shot.

Villas

On a detective's salary, I can't afford a vacation,
so I imagine it: April, advancing into
mountain light, the fake mountain light
in the back projection – Las Colinas: is that
the girl's address? Check the pocket book,
there's always a set of cultural references
people aren't aware of: uh oh, a date
with some guy... sex in an open field,
glowing under the full moon. What?
You say he's the police commissioner?
There goes my promotion. That journalist
was going to reveal it all: shut him down. You
post the gun to a college guy, I get off here,
the companion you can't see, who sees everything.

Subcontinent Nocturne

The atmosphere is breathless. People here
solve mathematical problems for a dime each,
philosophers sell peanuts on the street,
a monkey on a chain... all you can eat
for a dollar, you can buy a government official
for twenty bucks, and the only people smoking
are the prostitutes. The gaudy magazines tell
the young programmers to be on a cool team,
to demand a training that gets them
into the call centres full of money. A large
old domain is sold to the man in a blue suit.
But the town seems tedious on the trip back
from the airport – after California, it's a dump –
I hear the city's soulful call – don't leave me again.

Winter Maps

The cascades cascaded; so far so good, and
parts of Europe reminded me of the vineyards
whose wine tasted of the forest floor.
I wrote down the names of these areas,
and the list seemed both necessary and sufficient.
The whole experience was a kind of education.
In the Northern hemisphere, the April dawn
heralded spring, but not where I come from.
Lots of 'money' was signed over to me
on the video shoot, just to bamboozle the
audience. It wasn't counterfeit, but it had
no exchange value, in the crucial new store.
To open an account you had to be up early, and
answer this question: Are you a man or a mug-shot?

Whistle While You Work

If you whistle while you work, you can
make a living quoting Latin mottoes.
So he said. He had a quick drink
before the show, and will now resume
tickling the tonsils. 'Out there (beyond
the Black Stump) it's more peaceful, but
that can be boring, no?' You call that
dialogue? I prefer 'you' in the plural.
But to sit with you for a while... Oh,
you'd prefer someone more senior,
I see. So it's back to San Francisco, back to
the shadow of poverty, and the role in the play
where the old woman is seen committing a crime.
Catch her picking the pocket, and you win the prize.

Among Wild Swine in the Woods

He was on track for a promotion,
or so he thought. Clothes newly cleaned,
hair combed, shoes polished, he travelled to
Newcastle alone to do point guard duty.
It was an ideal union by the sea. Far below,
your loan for nearly half a million drifted;
now the law makes you into a zebra, an ass
with stripes. You'll learn to handle things.
The publisher grudgingly signed the clause
that the author insisted on. It's true
we have not avoided our destiny. We have to
clear the air. Literature being a kind of gas,
standing by the door at the book launch was clever,
in case you needed to get out of there.

Bracket Creep

The chief lender hears the turning of the year.
The investment advisors' advice, well, take that
with a grain of salt: they have a sweet little deal
there where the law was buyable, if you
had a million – do I hear two million?
And all that lot, gathered at the bar,
were mourning the death of capital.
To tell the truth the air turned to smoke.
I long for a clatter of high heels
on the steps. That is, a door opening
onto the real world outside the banking sector:
fresh air, sunlight and bird calls.
I wish I had sons and also
daughters to aim at a better future.

Bomber's Moon

Senator from the nuclear age,
our cages are no protection
in autumn's far country, all rusted and red.
I wonder if there is a non-nuclear future –
my ten-year diary says there is.
Chantal thought Julia was a pain in the neck
and for all the promises of dalliance, she was.
We're off to a party held by yours sincerely
on the ground floor; you can come, if you promise
to behave. There is a leading lady, and a hero
denounced by the mob, and it's probable
that our elected representatives don't give a damn.
No, I am not the son of the Senator, and clearly
not meant to fall into the vat of acid.

Drinking in the Kitchen

The economy took a while to recover.
All those executives rolling in our money,
like pigs in shit. Ugh! The night is cold
and delicate and full of angels. The Minister
of Finance is having some kind of fit. And so
we turn the page and start over again.
Go to London to buy a car, a Skoda:
the Polish workers are leaving for Europe,
they've had enough of cleaning toilets
after the executives have spewed in them.
That's reasonable, isn't it? What would you do,
rolling around in Poland with a wad of banknotes
with a portrait of Queen Elizabeth on each one,
stained, just a little, by vomiting executives?

Digital Clock

Victoria's receding song failed to call them in.
Nor did the wild song wallet call them out.
To our workforce, your brilliance is nothing more
than knowing what important details to ignore.
Write down what dictum is needed for the bit clock
on the new computer, at lift-off time.
A logic bomb lobbed into the research lab
will close it down for two years. Careers
multiplied in the dark, e.g. training the guards
to guard the trainers. He asked the prima donna
to sing again, and now you have gone quiet
like an audience that wants to be respected.
All the class crew were directed to whistle
just before interval. Now your time here is done.

Old Folk

So the poor people promptly ordered a hamburger.
The younger brothers came from the onyx land,
the country that was in the news because of its
atrocities. Before the story came the name:
the name of Graham Vick's 'Dunwoody
Housing Estate' for the elderly and confused,
where stubborn mathematical theorems are proposed.
So you're not happy with the scenery around here.
A stamp could reproduce all this in detail,
down to the last autumn leaf, the odd-looking smoke
drifting from the chimney, the car idling on the drive.
The born-agains are stuck on the 'don't believe it' routine.
And now the call to sit on the board of *La Compagnie
australienne:* they're all foreigners, but do what you can.

Cover Art

What happened here? We were promised
verdant vistas, no? But what dismal scene
is this? Bodies everywhere... you call this
a luxury hotel? Where I come from politics
means the ballot box, not the machine-gun.
As the Good Book says, when two or more of you
are gathered – it's not democracy, but it gets things
done. John Wayne would fix this mess pronto.
But behind that makeup... a tiny brain,
ticking over, slowly. One person, one vote...
why, that means... all those poor people, breeding,
next thing they'll be telling us... the voters
gathered in the hall told us how Norman Rockwell
invented America, just how they like it.

Bookkeeper's Holiday

On the train from _________ I read a long
short story and from border to border
clambered through an imaginary landscape,
the weather redundant though summery.
Then I read the reports of what Markham knew
and when he knew it, and how certain receipts
were 'lost' by Markham, who left 'The Firm'
in a hurry. Moths climb in the flame.
Ah, subtle Emilia, what's up? What caused
your convenient delay? One little Roman lesion,
and your body recycling the air. We found –
hidden in a locker – the books Markham took,
and the old law books too. The boss found them,
but he was not to hear the slaughter, on the CD.

Lady Mondegreen

Tea with Lady Mondegreen at one of those
classy places, candles, waitresses.
She won a thousand a month in a raffle
and on the spur of the moment banked it,
so it slowly aggregated and grew:
a bunch of digits quietly multiply
in the database as it updates annually:
checked, backed up, reified into cash.
Checking her diary of the war years – Paris,
well, she needed to erase some events:
one crazy for the bottle, a pillar of waiting,
betrayal, some of the group shot, at 1:00 p.m.
The report went to London, but in the horrors
of The Blitz, was anybody listening?

At Sans Souci

The young man appeared at breakfast, and said
he wanted to be a romantic poet, nothing more.
Success at that is little more than dust.
Curator of his own emotions, embalming
his memories while they were still readable,
scribbling, typing, buying and selling real estate.
Much later: 'All I want is a quiet talk,' she said,
and she sat smoothing her frock on her thighs.
'Displacement gesture', the textbook said, starlings
grooming their feathers. Sister Louise will see you
now: don't you want the massage? Louise wanted
more from the so-called poet, more emotional salt,
but he was all gesture, just a reputation,
empty hands and a 'mouth full of much obliged.'

Pride of Erin

All your home improvements may well
turn to vapour in the evening as the money drains
out of the market. You can sue, and you may win,
but you'll wait a long time for the money.
Trouble, that was something between her legs
and it sure made a mess of the accounts.
She and 'Mr Rayban' had that 'conversation'
then it broke up. Debt to assets, I mean.
You may recall that we were the life of the Bourse,
but not any longer. It never had a soul before.
Failure is one domain to wish well behind you.
Kindness is not necessary at the plant, and not
in the office, but when you look at the wreck
around you, maybe we were mistaken all along.

The Armani Endowment

You were born in an inauspicious year
when theory was on the rise in seminar rooms,
when old hands sought to reassure their colleagues.
They went quietly, in the end, then
didn't pollution arrive with the new song
and the Armani money and a young professor?
The great careers are like that, he said:
a bright burst, then a slowly fading flame.
His secretary confessed that she had met
'Graham' at the races, she'd put a thousand dollars
on 'Corn Lordship' and lost the lot, was this
love? It was enslavement, of a poor kind,
like a glass cross on a cheap necklace.
Live off it, Professor, and don't crack up.

Sheriff of Nothing

In his remote province his work was valued.
That lifted his spirits, his biographer notes
in a margin. Unsupported by reason's enigma
he wanted more but he didn't get it. Drat.
Sitting in a darkened room, typing, for decades –
a consultant of nothing, doing time. And
the servants are pleased to be enslaved, especially
the worn-out wife, carving the lamb for dinner.
His biographer was not likely to reveal
what his research turned up: infidelities,
greed, cruelties large and small. Now
he's writing the life of a Eurasian beauty
who lives beyond the law with a scrum of men.
Her daughter will do well in New Jersey.

Blue Moss

All she could be convicted of is a love
of luxury, and who could blame her?
Years in a camp, among the torturers
and the tortured, unsanitary sex for a cigarette.
No way is clear for escape. Eat your dinner,
or there won't be any more, her mother said.
Hide in the toilet or die for two sacks of coal.
There is no use trying to escape.
Don't argue over what to drink, just drink.
All year long we're poor, then we're middle-aged.
Finally a dawn crowded with American soldiers.
The dialogue was either a blip or a blunder.
The long clear arm of golden liquid turned into
spray, and the spray is a blue moss killer.

Break Some Eggs

A butler enters with a letter on a tray. Come in,
sit down on the sofa. It's always there.
The young woman belonged to no one,
she said, though she was married, strictly speaking.
It's not a good sign for the women on the jury
to laugh. That shows no respect
for the horrible murderer. Though perhaps
he's just a bystander, or a distracted passer-by.
Think of the huge debt your adventures last year
incurred while you were grovelling on your knees,
humiliating yourself in front of a female junkie.
In every pensioner there's a child crying
to be taken home. Nearly there, you said;
we're doing well in Omelette Park.

Muzzle Flash

Not able to make a clean break,
Jed hung around the town for months,
so it was said he had mammal delirium.
His wife and I had a near-miss one time
when he came rocketing out of the alley
at the back of the movie palace, blam! glimpse
of a gun muzzle flash, well, 'palace' gives the wrong
idea. You might as well ask a hog what is happening.
He would keep calling around for the letters
he wrote and gave to some youngster
to deliver. He would tremble in a bar,
or just hover above Munk Park, half alive.
The scene is a renowned beauty spot named
in honour of a Doctor Munk from Hong Kong.

Police Action

The years of ample pay are denied by Old Tom.
No one is willing, right now, to recall
the heights he scrambled to, trampling others.
And he was upset that his son hated him.
Oh well, the more you suffer, the stronger you are,
opined Liz, from behind a bottle of gin.
The old man really is something else, no?
What are the differences between these two
photographs? One is red, one is blue. And the face
resembled yours, the one reflected in the water.
Since the anguish of staff turnover bothers you,
take a holiday. While you're gone we'll
finish off the labour unions. In the cool dark outside,
whistling from the police took the form of sleep.

Smash and Grab

Sorry to keep you waiting, Ward. We have given
this whole business a great deal of thought.
It seems highly unlikely that you will ever
understand the depth of our grief on this issue.
It feels like post-natal depression, but with an edge.
Do you grasp that, dimly? But before we
put the knife in, do you have something more
to say for yourself? In your new script
a crazy film director follows a civil conflict,
right? The script is riddled with confusion,
like the so-called fog of war. Slowing down
opens out new avenues, and you will have time
for your silly hobbies – your Alamo, your
Waterloo – and you may yet learn to please.

Working the Oracle

Well, said the Senator, this week
let's do local cuisine, a slap-up dinner
at the Red Rose Café. No more theatre.
No more news from home while you're
deep in the crucible of capital: longhorn nausea.
The whole class took the offshore tours package
like some pocket history of the world, then
Holly won a dazzling victory over Carole Lore.
She now had the measure of the A Class:
it was due to what she learned in Vera Cruz.
From what the girl at the door said, Holly's
the courtier next in line, so select which senior
dinner companion you want, and listen:
he'll show you how to lose, or how to win.

The Tomb of Baudelaire

The governess did it; it was her mission.
Did the commissioner think she was beautiful?
It was just one woman, as cold as marble.
She did what she had to do, in her rapture.
Sure, she had allure, she nodded and winked,
and in the end she received justice. It did nothing
to improve things. What can you do
with what is still a mainly rural economy ?
Walsh said he would grant legal aid
but only for 14 weeks. Rick Thompson
was also bringing a gift of some kind.
We have moved on a little ahead of them.
On the last yards to the prison that song
was still within her, grazing, complete.

The Tomb of Edgar Poe

The mail is on holiday, my dear, but I shall apply
an ornate version of your name to the envelope.
The letter inside says that a famous poet
fetched you from Liverpool to London for some
disorderly conduct, the door locked and someone
in there fornicating, the linoleum floor
the scene of a historic union. Recalling
all you explained about how to kill a man
with a folded newspaper or a sharpened pencil,
it really dawned on me what a shit you were,
how one minute you see the fake shop-front
of the spy outfit, and then you don't, and in this
training pit leased out to the interrogation schools
the whole business starts to frighten even you.

The Tomb of Verlaine

Like a first-aid kit no one ever uses, here's
the tomb of a really famous pederast,
the guidebook says, lots of words inscribed
on the marble facing in ornate script,
unfortunately in some obscure tongue.
He wrote hundreds of aphorisms, it says,
one of them claiming to outlast bronze.
I don't see any bronze around hereabouts,
so maybe he was right. Did you see that blonde
who joined the tour in Brussels? What a dish!
She's a real doll, and the guide – senile galoot –
showed her how to give the knuckle-ball salute
to the Lords of the North, owners of that villa
we visited, the library stuffed with French poetry.

Well-equipped Men

Lately I've been looking at old-fashioned plaids.
I'm sure I deserve a beautiful suit. Call me,
before the Hong Kong tailor leaves town.
I love the popular songs from the fifties,
yet I shall never return to the past, that attic,
nor bid for the tawdry items that were on offer
from the poorest chamber-pot to the glittering jewel,
oh God, if we had been in clever Cleveland –
I would have voted for a dazzling uniform
in a silent room, and a loaded sawn-off shotgun,
sawn in half for a leading role in the documentary
about the muscly brothers in the rusting truck
on target for the abortion clinic: the news story
inflamed them and no one is responsible.

The Drunk at the Lecture

We would have lost a nuclear war
if one had happened, but I was busy
paying off my darling's credit cards, and
I wouldn't have noticed. The news bleeds
from one side of this great continent
to the other. Drab Gelman, that was his name.
He was often more formal than one needed to be.
Is that a sign of some deep inferiority?
When things went wrong he bounced back.
Everybody wondered who the new arrival was,
but he was just the old arrival in a suit, speaking
English well and Italian badly, the lingo of Leslie
the Offender. Laughing, I maintain her in the style
to which she would like to become accustomed.

Touch of Evil

Orson Welles made the movie, but the studio
cut it to shreds, and can you blame them?
They just wanted the thing to be very popular
and suck in millions of dollars. Walter Murch
dug up the old reels, and fiddled with
the sound effects, and bingo! Now
stare at the movie, look lovingly at that
famous tracking shot, it goes on and on
like an anaconda, dragging the audience in.
Marlene Dietrich a prostitute, can you believe that?
Then the work is redeemed by the sound effects
at the end and the audience can relax. Look –
snow. Is it winter already? How time flies.
Back to the fifties, when things were real.

Mister Real

It was known that the senior teacher might come
to the high school formal, despite the unspoken
taboo; he had a name for their bravado
and their girlish innuendoes, for he knew
nothing can bring a child undone more quickly
than the crash into adulthood via the glands
and a bottle of sugared bourbon and fizz.
The ambrosia had an awful lot to do that night,
for the kids were faded in the precise moment
of bursting into bloom. A few more years
and that cute blonde will be a harassed mother,
wanting magic English, a civil hello from Mister Real
from the slums, an end to the slanging matches,
and a private income to be spent only on champagne.

Liana

The constellations are rising in perfect order.
If you want a future, make a wish now.
Don't wring your hands and whimper;
bring the other near, and listen. He has
something to say to you. If you turn away,
more water flows under the bridge,
and it is your fault, stupid. That one
is a real handful, a Sherman Tank.
Despite his position, in the American lingo
he is lower than a pig in mud, and a minor criminal,
and a sordid creep as well. Choose one of the songs
that had hung around the fringes of the hit parade
from the Time of Methuselah: the Lithuanian dirge
they didn't want to use in *Oklahoma!*

Down by the Station

He knew he had to find a meal ticket.
The last racket was a turkey. Then the scene
changed, but intermittently, as through dark mist,
and he found that he had become fashionable.
He travelled up to his old college. So there he was,
week-long, the honouree and his gadget:
a shoulder holster with a spring release.
He should have met Leonard Woolf first thing
this morning at the station, but he was pie-eyed
and one of the servants had to do it. Last month
he placed the folded bribe in the blue envelope
and dabbed the back with a little honey
like a seal or a kiss. Now his filibuster accent
is on the evening news in the Year of the Dog.

Lateral Sclerosis

Small loans are the ruin of the older folk in
Country Antrim, but in nearby Muckamore
they're laughing. Mr Sillars went over them
carefully – we all want that reporter off-limits –
and the letter he provided for a signing-on fee
seemed valid. Getting the focus right is hard:
thirty dollars on the one hand, one billion euros
on the other: one hungry family is a tragedy,
a million a statistic. This information is useless.
I want to go back, out of the bad stories.
Be sure to include some of the rebels in the army.
And carry a gun. If they can put up with their comrades
their mournful future will take on a classical look,
like a military history getting ready to be recorded.

Bohemians en route

More people, less room. This motel sure has
a prickly atmosphere. The storm subsided;
the dwarf led you to the end of a street.
Her rehearsal of fear and alarm is an act,
learned beautifully in London back in the
fifties. Can we go back there, please?
Love for the cute animal is contagious.
One also has the infants to think about
as we circle around the small museum
which is really a 3-D colour diapositive
of the usual Mexican tourist trap, including
blue margaritas: sugar and salt on the rim
of a glass of hooch on the slippery table, and now
I am a two-man woman on the run.

Good Times

This is a great time for theology. Satan
is everywhere, which makes you optimistic.
A good opponent stirs debate. But if so,
she with her loud 'kill the money' rant
speaks more harshly than we need.
The soul has to stay where it is, where
the janitor hoovers a new home for the killer –
dial 911, quickly! Here they come:
a gang of Mafia thugs from Sicily where the
'pleure similar douceur' is kept for the tourists,
more than half of whom are full of drink,
calm and voluptuous as the poem says, where
calm is the effect of severe brain trauma and
very little tantalises the inner child.

Don Wan

A glass of champagne for luck and down you go,
under the wave, past the has-been losers
and someone called Monty: they are you,
in the mirror, at the end of another weary year.
You can't be blamed for giving up, when no one
comes to dinner – or she's the wrong one,
stumbling in through the hot-house full of
dying plants: armoured, calm and half-alive.
The more we feel deeply, the more we resemble
the shabby poet Nadir Longley in his long decline,
cadging drinks at dusk on the boardwalk.
For him, to abandon art would have made nonsense
of his long struggle. Thus there is no answer
to the problem of pathos vs. experience.

Emma

Today's Madame Bovary lives for the moment,
her study piled high with sexy books.
She wins the Backward Prize, and the news photo
shows her surrounded by chummy chaps all
nudging her onto the London gravy train
that dumps clubbable poets, bedecked with medals,
into the laps of the middle class. Write
wild and free, but don't frighten the buyers.
Emma's full of sense, and sensibility, she knows
how to do the persuasion, without seeming to.
There is one winning envelope and only one
ethical issue to face. She says 'I feel the carousel
starting slowly and going faster and faster!'
We are gone down into the land of the persuaders.

Deep Sky

In the hut by the tropical beach family values
are a stumbling block, and the lithe boys
leave them at home for the sake of the income
from the dirty old man who pays them to mix
his paints and just a little more, a sacrifice
of honour. Of course we know it happened
not quite by chance. Real artists are beyond
common middle-class morality. They say.
What cultural roost there is in this country
is ruled by schoolteachers and journalists,
Patrick White said. True; far away in Sydney
there had never been a cultural elite, and no
Sir Norman Hartnell and his hats and frocks.
Talent? It's relative. Sexual pleasure is the absolute.

Man Overboard

She got an ormolu cooler-cover from her daughter
and she only turned seventy on Monday.
The weather is warmer near the landmarks.
Was your name on the honours list? No,
I missed out again – like your first husband,
if that's any consolation. If there is a cure
I'll make the journey, up in the discreet lift
to the secret clinic; if not, not. Okay?
Four officers from the forum are here to see you,
madam. It's about the mail-order bride that
your second husband married, and the visa problem;
it is like watching a movie of a nightmare.
Working for a dollar an hour gets her
a green card and more useless literature.

Grace and Florence

When he's finished killing the East German
agent, ask him to report to the boss.
What exactly are those marks on the walls? Later
he came from all four corners of the future:
it was a conspiracy of right-handed notions.
We have been expecting you, Mister Bond –
we hope you have enjoyed the onshore breezes,
and the 3-D memory laugh behind the pool.
Sort through the list of Stasi agents; one of them
is highly placed in your office. No more will cygnets
lap the pond. You met the boss's wife? She's on her
awful downward spiral, drinking. Don't ask.
It's the mental inhaler again, while her
inflamed on-and-off romance becomes familiar.

King of the Hill

If marginal calls are made, the stock market
won't be able to handle it. It's less trouble
for them to pay someone to fix it, than
for them to fix it. You can tell the top brass:
they have a flower in the buttonhole.
A lovely pale blue check shirt, flax, linen.
And a kiss for the informer on your lap,
and for the boss, a stiff drink or two.
We are paying to stay for a while in your place –
is that okay? We'll get a cleaner.
She smoked heavily: one lung less for her,
and she's lucky to survive the operation.
King of the hill, for what that's worth. This
was mine, and I let it slip through my fingers.

Melting Moments

If you and that creep come in late for class
don't apologise, please. There's no point.
There never is. Staying up late, drinking
with the head teacher, watching him fall asleep,
you think you're immortal. For more years,
it seemed, than an omnivore has had
hot dinners, we sat watching the cute
New Zealander, one hand on her stomach
and the other holding a carving knife, although
that too is something that must be analysed,
together with the rest of the ugly drama.
On Friday at dawn Mêler will be there, full of
love for her and her song, and the envelope
full of powder, the reason for her lover's ennui.

No Parole

With that lot of tough-guy senior citizens it was
the Town of the Land Rovers. Men have a mystique
of their own, like women, but more mystical.
All the great religious madmen were mad men.
You call this a holiday? On the one hand,
the Romanian police, but then the local Mafia
are more gruesome. Is Pakistan any better?
If that Maori song disco dance planner, she said,
is on the train to Lahore, then I'm outta here.
She had been the script girl on a movie that won
all this year's awards. We strolled out of the movie
into the glare and noise of the street and she
started arguing about some Sondheim musical,
this event rounding the corner.

The Coloured Future

Left to their own devices they're has-been nobodies,
but when they're called, they're special. So they think.
Too bad they didn't ask my advice. It turns bitter
when the shit hits the fan and they're no longer news.
Heaven has no rage like children who are born
too late to a couple of homeless people, they
can kiss the idea of promotion good-bye. What causes
moonlight? Ask the top executive, Mister Shankar,
laughing alone in the top floor penthouse
high above the corporate maelstrom, who orders
all the rituals Colonel Bach instituted to be struck out
and replaced by one woman who wears a dress too tight
on all fours on the grass of the Executive Putting Green
while her children at home review their budding careers.

Monkey Business

I think we have a buyer for the Mall. Ask the boy
to take the other children down to the Cages and play –
oh, play Taunt the Mandrill. Bob wanted a hyena coach
to train the creatures to be usable patrol dogs.
We had an excess. The results are not lost on Bob,
who will call room service and not pay the bill.
Signs of rot and corruption are everywhere. His wife
hits the right note so that Princess Taekwando
combined with the Rush Limbaugh of oral argument –
read the 300-pound woman warrior, madly drinking –
can fall through the floor and still be the living
soul of the party, like a value within the worksheet
that has the code to cancel the other calculations
so that the sale of Fallbrook Mall collapses.

Chinese Chequers

Catholics are lucky: people pray for them.
The watt bulb awareness of all your computers
added together will compile a loose description
of your fate, and the nuns will sit and read it.
You will pull the issue from a pool of hundreds –
the most remarkable, and also the worst – and present it
to the youngster who says that the cinema fumble
was outside the normal range, and with a bigger thrill.
A sketch of your life would look like a mirror
held up to your future, where the good times
written backwards end nowhere. Don't they anyway?
Yet you are the reward rejected by that career.
From where I sit I can see hundreds of freight cars.
You will find, in that vista, all you could have been.

Aqueduct

A storm in the Fall soaked the muck. The jockeys
flailed around the track like silken butterflies.
All races that are not fixed will play like this.
Schultz insisted that the horse was not a fake. Now
the patient listener uses the upper deck of an era
to spot the cheats through binoculars, some kind of cop.
In her role as an innocent, little Miss Nicole Milburn
put the money on for her mother Tilly the Killer.
The fact that you are the one who owns the horse
and fails to keep your one eye on the ball won't
impress the judge, said Officer Derek Reasoner.
He had a script from 'The Bulldog' to work through:
'You should have played the knuckle-ball scenario
and offered a tip to the gentlemen in the bullpen.'

Davy Jones

You're not so virtuous, Jim. Edgar Hoover
has a grainy photo you should see: some figure
in fishnet stockings, a guy, fer crissakes! He says
there's something about the turn of the ankle...
all else is shadow. And way beyond
the reach of the law a diminutive woman –
Barbie, of the Musketeers – gently pushes open
a security door, a flashlight held in her teeth.
Is that John Paul who enters silently behind her?
The Senate deleted the accusations from her file.
... as though the story could advance its pawns.
In your filing cabinet they found a pencilled note,
a pair of stockings... would that connect you to her?
Two pirates lower the flag and fold it away.

Honeymoon Hotel

It's good for her to know that the Brochure
is a major work. Put it right here, where
the boss has to look at it every morning.
Make an announcement: say that anyone,
even that smelly derelict the boss's brother,
can turn up and guzzle the cheap wine.
People stoned on weak coffee write to us.
Gawkers perpetuate the misquoted line.
We're checking the local mall cinema where
motion occurs all night long in the rows of seats.
On the screen a man floats over Niagara Falls,
then plunges down like a human cannonball.
Okay, we're drinking cheap whisky from a bottle
in a paper bag, would you put us in jail?

Bridge in the Rain

The dream (plan, outline) has a moment when
a truck driver is misled: the Wilson Bridge
appeared as some generous little connector road
when really disaster waited; the will of a killer
reified on a dirt road. On the radio, is the blond
goddess really a young goddess? She was in fact
remarkably old, and mainly muscle and gristle,
tap-dancing the yellow brick road to fame.
In her argument against the worship of bourgeois art
she uses her numbness as evidence. Then on her journey
to the Wild West, a crow appeared in the train,
banging into the windows, name of 'Baron Corvo', and
his harsh warning is this: the moonlight, the night,
the sleeping animals – it all gets carted away.

So Long

Go meet the lenders in Polk Street Park,
and you had better bring them their money.
Watch for a guy wearing headphones
parked and listening in a distant vehicle.
The girl meets the guy, they stroll in the crowd,
talking out of the sides of their mouths.
The 'old mom' rule will limit how far
you can employ the Ramon Switch Trick.
Out past the two-mile limit there are bodies
rotting in a magma pit of boulders beyond
federal jurisdiction. Who will get rid of them?
The perfume climbs into my tree, saying
the rat race originated with the nipple.
The mournful radar is a blanket over me.

News Item

The poet's character was moulded on that of the more
bizarre children who were human, granted,
though not one of them had a single emotion
and the rest were wizards. Whistle and you'll fly,
was their motto. They will spice up the news
with their coup. I prefer the channel where
Senator Dole likened a military manoeuvre to a
football ploy. I shall return in the dark and be seen.
Add this: Doctor Waldo misses the mark
and the law misses the risk of a mad bomber,
sick with anger because he is without a job.
He eats his slops without benefit of knife or fork.
He is hoping he'll be a major news item
on the nine o'clock news, tonight, in New York.

Hair of the Dog

Wake up, you're looking at this magazine, in which
an old woman blows bubbles in her local
swimming pool below the water mark,
far from her comfortable home and relatives.
She is surely the Republican who worked on
a method of deregistering Democrat voters
in slow motion. I was told to use the locker to
write this up, far from my local home folder.
On my lonely travels I will miss the Upper Bay
inbound crew, their happy work songs –
some women were complaining about the songs,
how they spread moral doubt and communism.
Read the tone of voice: when the guy who owns
a big truck speaks, get off your bike and listen.

At the Movies

Caliban

Leslie Neilsen, Prince of Brylcreem, steers
his spaceship through a field of sound effects
to the forbidden planet. Why is he there?
To romance the Professor's nubile daughter whose
air of innocence hangs around her like a perfume.

She keeps a pet tiger. Leslie gives a manly frown
at the unspoken threat: when the girl
becomes a woman, the tiger will kill.

It's what the Wild West looks like circa 1956,
or *The Tempest* in outer space with rum and Coca Cola,
with a well-bred English scientist running things.
What do they talk about in the studio canteen
between takes? A tip for Saturday.

Darkness falls, and innocence, and the hideous id
is banished to the caves deep under the ground
where the abandoned machines hum
all night long and an invisible monster
stumbles through the night to threaten them all.

Jack will ruin
his master.

Columbo's Kangaroo

Detective Columbo is questioning a clever murderer
who is a magician in his day job, with his own
television show. Here we are in the back lot,
sun beating down, between the villain's
trailer and the waiting studio, a script in his hand. 'Oh,
just one more thing, sir,' says Columbo, preparing
a subtle query to slip in between the man's ribs
and drain the blood from his heart – 1976 –
and we notice, a hundred yards away, between
two hangar-like studio buildings, an actor
in a Roman Centurion costume, smoking
and talking to a friend, and beside him
a kangaroo on a lead looking around
then tentatively sniffing the ground.

The Last Clean Shirt

We have to make do with Third Avenue,
which is a street in an urban environment.
It runs parallel to Second Avenue, naturally,
because parody means parallel discourse.
The spectator is trapped, and we are shown
a 'Walk' sign. Do they shirk the issues? No,
they just find more elegant ways
to engage ethical issues. Okay, shirk the issues.
Then you have some guilt, and where to put it?
Would you like a weekend in Havana?
Maybe for the music, but the politics?
We could bring some fiction: fiction could at least
be subversive. You won't be bored
and you won't be lazy. Elke Sommer
and Loretta Young shine. Can the escape hatch
be found within Frank O'Hara's subtitles?
'I used his lines against the image,'
the cinematographer said. Does he mean that he,
Alfred Leslie, subverted the subtitles?
Or the image? Can we trust him? He's
talking about 1964, more or less.

So there is a struggle, hidden from the audience.
Which force takes over? No, they only
stress their differences. They would like to
make something new appear
on the surface of the screen, moving, childish.
Then it seems that many of these subtitles
are direct quotations of poems. Well,
what did you expect? It is a secret anthology,
a mask of Frank O'Hara. He often moved

from one type of writing to another. No,
he never shied away from whetting his language
against other media.

Here's a strange contradiction: how to display
an excess of sight, and then tact. And although

there are connections with death and dying,
no shirt is ever mentioned.

In the end, we have been taught
not to take things at face value:
we are now free to walk by ourselves,
we have completed our training in skepticism.
Huh. Here are some fantasy bribes,
offered by the manipulators of desire.
They can't help it if they are well financed.

Maybe you could attach your guilt to Mother,
or perhaps World War Two. Frank
fought in that. I just hope the rain
won't wash it all away.

Rink

The opening scene is shot outdoors in bitter cold:
bottle-blue dusk, which she sweeps through
more or less like a swift or a swallow, shaving whispers
off the surface of the road, that is, the ice vault
over her private black glass underworld.
The arena is bordered by rushes and canes
and just over there a shred of plastic.
Now this mise en scène is not
a commercial franchise, so no soft drink cans
or teenagers, likewise a lack of maintenance,
no surface grading, brushing or injury insurance, and
you also have to imagine, if you wish to track
cause and effect, an erratic anti-depressant routine
and a shouting husband in a trailer-park
a decade ago, half forgotten. A bird swoops by
to draft a reconnaissance whose terms
are kept from us, then dodges away.
The ice is not evenly thick, and the sky
is tending to a twilight deeper than the ice
and so two linguistic fields overlap: grey cloud,
an inscribed surface too mottled to be a mirror,
too dangerous to offer praise, echoing
the other backdrop, her various failed careers
including wife, mother, star of the rink.

The Glass Bottom Boat

As the boat noses out into the bay the History
of the Western World unrolls below, and
scientist Rod Taylor imagines he can see,
reflected faintly in the glass floor, the panties
of the female guests, this vision
from the unconscious of the mass movie audience
superimposed on a world of little fish.
The director quickly changes the design of the boat;
all Rod can see now are the fish below,
through a window enclosed in a plywood apron,
and all you can hear above the squeals of the children
are the jokes: simple, harmless and American.
An actor makes a meal of a dish of transistors,
and the future of the race is foretold in this
brainless entertainment and no one cares.

Inside Doris Day is a little girl
trying to get out: Doris Kappelhoff,
freckled kid from Ohio. Take a trip
to the blue room or the red room. Rod deprives her
of the bottom of her mermaid suit,
looking for panties again. Perhaps she is a spy.
Part of the set was recycled, the modern part.
Santa Catalina Island is famous for water and boats.
These are large, comfortable vessels, they visit
the Lover's Cove Marine Preserve. These are windows
to another world. Among the kelp forests
a group can charter the boat at night.
Poor Doris, she was like an uprooted tree
swirling through the eye of a tornado, one viewer feels,
an aquatic Dorothy Gale in a gale. Then
she married again and again, but America
is sleeping safely with its secrets in the Western night.

Boy in Mirror

First words: Gimme your hand! Then a fall, a death.
I left town in 1957 and went away, boarding school
gymnasium whirring sixteen millimetre movies:
Escape From Colditz or *Stalag Seventeen*, blondes
with heaving breasts were *verboten* for good reason.

So what do boys like about vertigo? It was
a way of experiencing something alien and new:
we had a trick of breathing much too fast for too long
then another boy would squeeze your chest from behind
as you held your breath and almost burst
and a million years later you would come to,
on the floor of a room on another planet
surrounded by strangers while your memories
converged slowly like a crowd at an accident.

Picnic was strong enough, when I was thirteen;
Vertigo would have finished me off.

Now I can face Madeleine in the water in a suit,
her stiff blond hair and stilted accent and demeanour.
The wounded boy in the water quickly becomes a man
dragging her backwards behind him as he swims
to the shore at the foot of a huge bridge –
trying not to bruise Kim Novak's
wonderful tits.

Wounded three times, each time deeper
but he doesn't know yet what horrors...
what mistakes, misunderstandings... he's
juggling with a walking stick, he's toppling
off a chair.

But he must have seen her stark naked!
Not glimpsed yet: if only he knew: Judy
from Salinas in the mid-West, stormy gateway
to the land of Oz, hiding two secrets,
loose, human,
but also art, and also dragged into a willed shape

by a troubled man
 – restored in 1996 –

a footloose male: another in *North by Northwest,*
a direction no compass has ever known,
despite Hamlet's ham-fisted play-acting:
'I am but mad north-north-west –'
cut off from their normal jobs and bonding rituals.
Both women are imprisoned by a monster, though
the heroes don't realise that. First
we have to follow and then rescue the princess,
unmask or defeat the monster, awaken the sleeping beauty
to our desires and needs, but the women are awake
already to their own desires.

Cherchez la femme, then the action
moves to a strangely threatening rural arena
far from the city: dangerous heights and fatal falls;
the (blonde) is unfaithful to the hero, maybe because
she has been captured and possessed by another monster
and soon the hero is a cuckolder and the woman adulterous
and thus fallen, or falling, or dead and gone. We hear
some moody music – Bernard Herrmann's
more insistent music: all right,
I'm afraid of the future.

The first incarnation of the goddess is Madeleine,
a name in search of lost time, and quickly dunked, and
hailing from the East she is naturally cold
and remote in a steel-grey suit: now
she drives an English car, a Jaguar with plates that say
MGK 159, obliquely hinting at a stray fact
just outside the camera's field of view: the owner of the car
once owned an old MG type K sports car,
then got rich
and traded in the clunker for a Jaguar –
but kept the plates – they always want
some memento of their lost youth, and now
an actress plays with his new toy, pretends to drive it, but
we never see her driving, just getting in and out.

#

Later she can be
more authentic, working in a job,
where she absolutely must clock on until Mister Handsome
becomes pitiful and pleading. She might become
'Judy' from some dump in Kansas
and wear sloppy clothes. Anything's possible.
Speak like a tart, Judy! Good girl! Now she
walks on foot.

Earlier, locked in her metallic suit –
the wounded hero at the start
quickly spiralling into madness –
the mirror shape of the plot and counter plot
in harmonic motion, the circular corsage,
the spirals in the trunk of a dumb tree, then
the camera notices her hair, and the clumsy portrait,
driving in diminishing circles around the sunlit town.
Spiral, circle, spiral, circle...

May I commend the awkward acting? 'You
were the copy, you were the counterfeit –
those beautiful phoney trances' – thus
more sincere, or just less competent –
rather that than be like the brittle professional woman
in *North by Northwest*, or is that just a personal reaction?

And the smooth villain in the suit is named Elster,
German for magpie, a collector of beautiful things, but:
Die Elster stiehlt, so gut sie schwatzt – the magpie
steals as well as it chatters. So the great painter Elstir
haunted Proust – so much success! Yet
troubled by thoughts of his future death –
'ambitious melancholy clouded his brow' –
a clever analysis of a fleeting expression, which
may have been, in fact, the painter's embarrassment
at hearing a gushy and pushy young suck-up artist
praise his 'fame'.

So, Marjorie Wood says of her brassiere: 'principle
of the cantilever bridge, an aircraft engineer
down the peninsula designed it, in his spare time.'

Between two deaths – Gimme your hand!
and a good policeman falls to his death
in the alley below, then the old college chum Gavin –
Mission number, skid row? No, 'Colour, excitement,
power, freedom' – San Francisco eighteen forty-eight –
then Ernie's Restaurant with its red velvet wallpaper
and her green English car – in the Spanish Mission
graveyard calla lilies – mist fogging the lens –
a suicide's grave in consecrated ground? What
madness is that? Catholic continuity girl, please!
Then at the McKittrick Hotel, an old drudge:
'I've been right here all the time, putting olive oil
on my rubber plant leaves', then
a detour to the Argosy Bookshop and
an avuncular European man – if he reads books,
he must have glasses and a funny accent, then
a strange darkness falling too swiftly, following
the script into a kind of nightfall, however wrongly.

The scene in the redwood forest.
Her big white coat, so vulnerable...

Scotty (drinks) Boy, I need this!

There's a brandy bottle. Next scene:
Scotch and soda.

Fluffy white coat!

Pink soft body underneath!

Scotty: I always thought you were wasting your time
in the underwear department.
Good Barbara: Well, it's a living.

Kim Novak, left-handed, writing a sad letter:
We had fun... and then you started in on the clothes...
Beside her crummy hotel, the Twelfth Knight bar.

She had to die...

I hear voices...

God have mercy!

Paris Blues

It's the early sixties: before heroin,
before herpes and AIDS ruined things,
before the women's movement.
Jack Kerouac is still alive, though only just,
with eight years left to live. But

let's leave America behind and take
a cultural detour down to the cellar
where a successful American export,
a jazz band, is winding up for the night.
The hero is a nice guy: short back and sides,
casually dressed in slacks and a neatly pressed
polo shirt. You'd like him. He plays a trombone.
A trombone? But first

we see a city at dawn: a man wearing a beret
idling along the cobbled street on a push-bike
then a girl wearing a scarf and carrying
one of those long loaves of bread
in her basket, bought at a local bakery!
It must be Hollywood: and it is! Though
with a French savoir-faire and a touch of
je ne sais quoi. As we get used to the silky
black and white, and the smooth lighting, we realise
we have been drawn into one of those indoor-
outdoor binary universes: when the action happens
indoors, the lighting is perfect, a studio in Burbank, say,
where even in the phoney park the light is just right.
But in the 'real' outdoors it's windy and overcast
and the lighting is kind of muddy and
the passers-by look suspicious and distracted,
so it must be Paris, or a version of it.
Yes, in a dive in Paris the hep cats are jumping,
jiving like it was the forties, when in fact
rock'n'roll has come and gone, JFK
is President, and the Ford Edsel is old hat.
Then we see the hero's name: Ram Bowen.
Can they be serious? A name like that,

and Paul Newman with a trombone? Well, this is
a Paris of the mind, where ordinary suffering humanity
get to be pushed around by a bad script, so
anything can happen. The hero's buddy is a black guy,
but he's played by Sidney Poitier and wears
a suit and tie and a wristwatch and a short haircut,
so he's all right – however deeply touched by
the madness of art – that is, jazz entertainment.

Then two women arrive on holiday:
one white, divorced, with two kids back home,
and the other black and single. So we have
four Americans in Paris but with angst
instead of fun: these jazz dudes may be polite
and press their shirts, but poor Ram:
his struggle with the demon of art and all those
late nights make him despondent.

So through the sets of matched doubles
day after day the Jane Austen problem
keeps rearing its ugly head: ladies,
how do you catch your man, when he's
a wild free spirit who suffers for his art?

Of course there's a resentful older woman
with a French accent: we see her checking the till
in the cellar at daybreak when the crowds have gone,

and cooking, but she keeps to the shadows,
nursing her hurt beauty behind a veil of makeup.

We get a clue as to why Ram is a musician,
not a writer: Paris is picaresque, he says.
His new girlfriend Lillian misses this,
or maybe gets it and neglects to correct him,
shaking her blond hair, straightening her gloves,
waving her handbag at the expensive scenery,
thinking – perhaps – that picaresque is French
for picturesque, and not wanting to
put the kibosh on a blossoming affair:
the guy's Paul Newman in mufti, after all.

#

Meanwhile Sydney Poitier has a tormented talk
with his dusky lady friend Connie: colour,
the question of colour, that he can avoid in Paris.
Should he go back to New York and face it?
The colour problem that brave Americans are
painfully working through, white and black alike,
maybe it's his duty: she says it's his duty
until his teeth ache, but then she says
she wants to have dozens of children.
What's a guy supposed to think?

Ram wakes up late from the hangover of music.
He and Lillian have long talks about how
art eats you up, and we note that Ram
wears his wristwatch to bed, perhaps needing to time
what happens between those pressed white sheets.
As dawn breaks over tourist-flavoured Paris
he yawns and rises, his hair perfectly combed.
How can you tell if a man's art is authentic?
Why, opines the lady, it's the way he made me feel.
She speaks to him of Ram Bowen in the third person,
and addresses his dimple, which broods in silence.
Honey, he insists, I live music, morning
noon and night! Meanwhile her outfits
are astonishing: one beautiful coat after another,
scarves, gloves, hats: the product of resourceful
shopping as wide-ranging, committed and passionate
as Ram's devotion to his trombone.

Yes, Ram is hitched to his mournful trombone
and we have the feeling that one day
he'll find himself alone with the thing,
an old couple who don't much like each other.

'We are the night people!' the nicely-dressed
black man exclaims on the tourist boat,
'and it's a whole different world!' Sidney
is hinting at a kind of underground where
moral values are reversed, where being cool
is better than being prosperous and where art

has usurped Mammon's place on the altar.
Then he checks his watch and adjusts his tie
and the illusion breaks up into ripples.
He's a type, not a person, a vacant role
waiting to be imitated and filled in,
a cool black dude with the race problem
and a stern girlfriend to worry about.

They play some music as an interlude
from the dialogue, though for Ram
we know that this view is back to front.
Now why is that saxophone playing second fiddle
to a trombone? Have you ever seen a band
with a dominant trombone? Is it because
Paul is more handsome than Sidney?
Taller? More white, let's say? Then
we are asked to believe that Louis Armstrong,
America's ambassador of cultural goodwill,
is some great giant of modern jazz, oh please,
gimme a break, he was briefly avant-garde
before the Great Depression, long ago,
and the furious God of Bop has long since
consigned him to the dustbin of history
and the lounge rooms of the middle class.

Now Ram's pal the coke fiend is snorting heavily –
it's his way, he says. Well, he's a French Gypsy,
not a regular guy. Now Ram makes him
see his future in the figure of an old friend
ruined by drugs, busking on the street,
drooling and plunking on a tuneless guitar.
Gypsy, see a doctor, Ram says earnestly,
suddenly the concerned bourgeois. Then
more tourist epiphanies – shopping and kissing –
and as Ram hugs his blonde under an umbrella
an abashed camera coyly looks down
at his slacks and highly-polished casual shoes.

In this cloudy autumn weather they
cast no shadows, like devils, and *chez nous*

read the *Herald Tribune* just to keep in touch.
In the corner, a television set. This movie
might well appear there, titled *The Tender Trap*.
Sidney goes crazy with love and buys
more flowers than he can afford.

Then Ram meets a powerful agent
who knows everything – Ram is good,
but his music is not good enough,
says the wise man. That's an opinion,
but not a life plan. What to do? Being moody,
that's not suffering, you have to be a bastard
like Rimbaud. He used to keep lice in his hair
so he could flick them at passing priests, and
for a while there he was a sodomite –
no blondes for him – and when he got moody
he killed a man by throwing a rock at him,
and in the end he tore up his talent
and left all that art shit behind. So, Ram,
marry the blonde or the junk or the trombone,
just quit pissing around, will you?

At last Lillian comes to rest in her hotel room,
exhausted by her efforts to persuade a dumb guy
to marry her, in a wilderness of dishevelled suitcases
and loose shopping. Then he turns up, then
he has an attack of gloom and abandons her.

Oh, Ram! You and the scriptwriter both
seem to have lost your grip at the climax:
a more authentic person has taken over
and inhabited this blonde like a virus and
as the train for Le Havre chugs out of the station
in a cloud of steam I realise that Lillian
is smarter and more fun than Ram, and maybe
she's better off alone on the boat train heading
back to New York and her two kids, where Frank O'Hara
has just finished his poem 'Lana Turner has collapsed!'
on the Staten Island ferry on his way to a reading
in a snowstorm, and some other different and
more interesting movie is about to begin.

The Cedar Bar, NYC, 1957

Her name's McPherson, Laura McPherson. Married,
age late thirties, two kids. She's still pretty,
the bartender thinks. Some young guy
in a raspberry sweater is chatting her up
and smoking all the time.
She's studying art, by the look of the folder
which she clumsily bumps against his arm
so he spills his drink. She offers to buy him another.
No, he'll buy. Gin martini, straight up, with an olive.
'No, I won't show them to you,' she says, 'It's
too dark in here. This is the third time
you've tried to do a line on me, do you come here
every Thursday?' She's usually there Thursdays
after her art class, while her sister minds the kids.
She might live in the suburbs, but she has seen
enough life, thanks, for example, an old guy
who loved her was shot dead, by her husband.
Blood everywhere, and a broken clock. But it was
you or him, sweetie, so the detective said –
Mark, her husband – once he had shot him dead
and the cleaners had cleaned up the mess.
Waldo was the old guy's name, heart full of murder,
but so stylish you wouldn't believe it. 'Laura,
you are the better part of myself,' he had said,
then he pulled out the shotgun. She can't help
thinking about the good times she had,
back then, at that fancy advertising agency,
and look at her now, kids underfoot,
trying to make do on a policeman's salary. But
she still has talent, or so the instructor says.
She has a book in her bag to read
on the subway: *On the Road*. 'Oh, that,'

her new friend says, "I know the author.
Nice guy when he's sober. He got drunk
at a party, and called me a fairy, out loud."
"That's terrible," Laura says, and tastes her drink.

Contre-Baudelaire

The fifty-six poems in the last part of this book – from 'Albatross' to 'Landscape' – were written as a group in Italy in late 2009. They echo, respond to and sometimes argue with some poems from Charles Baudelaire's Les Fleurs du mal.

Albatross

Sometimes, to amuse themselves, the authorities
bring to heel corporate high-flyers – those
clever executives, men of many devices,
who play exuberantly with Other People's Money
and heap themselves with salaries no one could
ever spend in a lifetime of profligacy –
and arraign them in the dock.

Accused of nothing more than clever cheating –
wouldn't we all, given half a chance? –
these kings of the sky falter and mumble.
That brain like a steel trap that could easily recall
a shift in their investments of half a point
months ago, among a welter of obscure trades,
now struggles to remember who said what
about some crucial deal a week ago.
Their mantra – 'nice guys finish last' – which means
'I'm an arsehole, and I always win' –
shrinks to 'I'm afraid I can't recall' –
gourmets who could count off every vintage
from the north slope of an obscure vineyard
in the south of France now struggle to recall
a deal involving several billion dollars.

That shark of the market, how daft he seems now,
how frail and elderly, among the silks
who nag and worry at his list of crimes. The poet
resembles this prince of the open skies: when
forced to get a job and earn his keep
the poet's dreams, entangled with his giant ego,
turn him into a blundering buffoon.

Venus

Gothic girl, nightclubber, speed queen,
when the icy north wind rakes the streets
and you stumble home to your claustrophobic room
and find the heating cut off, what will you do?
A shot of something will warm your guts for a while,
then the bottle's empty, and the alien at the store
won't give you credit any more. Rummage in your bag:
garbage, more garbage, and an empty syringe.
You might get work in soft-core porn, perhaps;
or a job in a fly-by-night shoe shop, or a temp position
typing up bullshit for a junior sales executive,
or maybe you could try a standup comic routine,
learning to handle the hecklers and get a laugh
exposing your miserable life for a share of the take.

The Bad Writer

University administrators once respected poets:
portraits of Rimbaud in the cafeteria
and Coleridge in the Common Room inspired
student and lecturer alike to feats of imitation.
In those days the arts of literature flourished
and more than one critic, forgotten today,
enthralled by the loony bin, doss-house or graveyard,
glorified the life of poverty with garlands of roses.
My soul is a garbage dump where – lazy teacher,
vain critic – I groan and mutter to myself.
No paintings here, no music in the smelly dark.
Oh lazy days! Scribbling with a stub of pencil
I compose an epic of dirty sex and dissolution
that will top the charts and make me filthy rich!

Elevation

Above the factories, the steelyards, the golf links
laid out like a child's game, above the plots
of the canals and the plans of swimming pools
you rise with the morning sun and the other
successful bankers in First Class, above
Bangkok or Dubai, en route to that
restaurant at L.A. International – the one with
lava lamps and sullen waitresses – The Encounter,
where Coke is dispensed through buzzing ray-gun tubes
and banquettes afford the time-rich visitor
views of the planes and runways – designed, you
tell your friends, by Paul Williams, African-American –
in your linen summer suit you move with ease
through the lobby of the Honolulu Hilton;
winter on the Unter den Linden sees you strolling,
in camel-hair overcoat, with cigar; like a
swimmer you plunge through a gallery opening,
parting the crowd who are only there to admire you,
your virile joy so perfect it is quite beyond
adequate expression, so you bottle it up inside you
to mature like a Château Margaux '98 –
eighteen ninety-eight, that is – to be decanted
in your suite overlooking Sydney Harbour –
the Opera House lit up, a call-girl dozing
under the covers – the bliss of those celestial regions,
high above a fluttering exchange rate, beyond the lame
investment paradigms of lesser mortals, that
beach in the sky, above the jet stream, above
the Aurora Borealis and its fake curtains of light –
the bliss whose fizz ascends like a skylark's aria
high above the mud and filth of the Bourse.

Friends in Hell

When Hemingway finally dropped off the twig,
his carcass wrecked by drink and other problems,
he stepped into the boat and flipped Charon a tip
and sat in the back with a flask of Cuban rum.

Exposing their breasts and their naked flanks
would-be actresses twisted and writhed, still
hopeful of a role, apart from the casting couch,
and moans and whimpers followed them.

Kissinger, in the flickering dark, was demanding
the fame due to him; Nixon buttonholed the dead,
groaning on the shore, pointing out to them
the journalists who had hunted him from office.

Pale with grief, Marilyn, dazed and skeletal,
clung to her treacherous President, once her lover,
and begged of him a final, parting smile
as kind and sweet as his initial promises.

Stein – erect, dressed in black – stood
like a statue at the helm, her eyes fixed on
the bow cutting the black tide, but Hemingway
stared at the wake disappearing into the dark.

The Age of Nakedness

Do you think the Ancient Greeks and Romans
ran around with nothing on? Nice thought:
like their painted statues, gaudy, overdone,
they dressed only in lipstick and eye shadow
and had sex with anyone who took their fancy.
Imagine! Fucking by the open road!
In a back alley! At the café table!
And with the winter mists chilling
their skin to a skein of goose-pimples,
they shivered and exulted like health fanatics.
Women's nipples, it seems, were available
to any fellow with a thirst, like those public
drinking-fountains you see in shopping centres.
And the men – athletes, all of them –
their rippling pectorals invited licking
and lots of bites and kisses, lucky guys!

Just thinking about that golden age
when you visit a nudist colony, say,
why, it gives you the horrors: instead of
gods and goddesses posing for a sculptor
or a bodybuilder flexing his biceps for the crowd
you find a Diane Arbus world of freaks:
flabby dwarfs and gangly skeletons,
clerks who would look far better in a suit,
housewives who should wear housecoats
out of doors, their flesh pale and quivering
like blancmange, teenagers like dugongs.

The Age of Mechanical Reproduction
has a style of looking good that's all its own:
fashion models as skeletal as stick insects,
men like hyenas or packs of rabid dogs,
and that lazy look that junkies flaunt,
blanked out in a vacant doorway.

#

Beyond all that, though, children,
yet to reach the wastelands of adulthood,
still have a pure kind of energy; clear eyes,
bright laughter, a way of being astonished
by little things: a tractor, a running fox,
a harbour full of boats.

Lights on the Hill

Stanley Spencer, odd and British to the nth degree,
prowler of backyard allotments and annunciations
where life bursts from the earth and washerwomen
hold the secret of eternal life in their bosoms;

Fantin-Latour, who gathered a salon of poets –
nonentities mostly, except for Verlaine and his catamite,
some beautifully dressed for posterity, some *bohemién*,
mostly poseurs, one who doesn't give a fuck,

Bacon, emergency ward filled with screams,
one victim choked by a giant crucifix, one
sodomised in the Love Hotel, and wrestling apes
whose prayers and howls rise from a river of shit;

Rockwell, recording angel of an ideal suburbia
with the crime, the sex and the betrayals
painted over, an impasto of kindness
as thick as ice-cream, dream merchant, liar;

Picasso, leaping from the frying pan of a style
into the flames of another – equally horrible and
just as saleable in the end – priapic satyr urinating
on the highway of fame, leave us now;

Pollock, growing through cowboy masks, then
breaking away into a storm of interior decoration,
seeking out punch-ups and boozy philosophy,
dancing from beer to whisky to sex to death;

Whiteley, touched by privilege and early talent,
spoiled by the flattery of journalists and women,
lured to the flame of Manhattan and suffocated
by that vast, bland indifference of America;

Warhol, talented window-dresser, scheming
salesman, ringmaster of dizzy weaklings,
Emperor of Nothing, self-connoisseur –
excuse me, your five minutes are up –

These curses, these futile blasphemies, these
hangovers larger than the Brooklyn Bridge,
sobs, headaches, hissy fits, pissing competitions,
they are a kind of veterinary vitamin injection,

fit to raise a snoring draught-horse to his duties,
they are the mirror images of models
on the catwalk, the scream of a sleepwalker
waking as she plunges from a hotel balcony,

the pop of flashlights and the flicker of television,
these heaving delusions, fame regurgitated,
inspire us all with a passion to be impassioned
and spend our lives in the dying glare of journalism.

The Enemy

My youth was a shadowy cyclone, brilliant winds,
ragged clouds torn by a ray of sun, and now
the storm has made a ruin of an orchard
where I had hoped there might be fruit.
Autumn arrives, and the wind is sharp and chill.
Time to get out the rake and shovel
and try to make something of what's left:
dirt, and potholes full of grey water.
I'll plant a few dreams in the gravel, ones
that produce tiny, pastel flowers: maybe
they'll find the trace elements they need.
But patient time waits to devour everything,
gnawing at the roots of our lives: our enemy
that grows stronger as we sink to our knees.

Rotten Luck

To put up with a career as pointless as this,
it takes the courage of a gambler.
Okay, someone has to do it, but
like they say: *vita brevis, ars longa.*
The grave I look for is covered with brambles,
on a lonely hill in the bush. Jazz began
by livening up a funeral march. So
mix more drinks, and mix them stronger.
More than one winning lottery ticket lies
forgotten in a drawer. Dentists ply
their skilled and painful trade, ignored.
Many an opium poppy flaunts its
spangled petals in a silent jungle glade,
far from addicts, that babbling horde.

Correspondences

Nature is a city in which giant trees
speak in whispers; commuters pass there
through forests of advertisements
which plead and beg and stare with greedy eyes.
Like the long echoes from a distant traffic jam
where diesel truck and Vespa mingle their exhausts,
like a dark bar with the lights out, as bright as neon,
radios, magazines and billboards all agree.
There are jingles as harsh as the stares of children,
as glittery as glockenspiels, as brown as beer,
– and other ads are corrupt, cloying, brassy,
their vacuous tunes echo in the mind forever,
like whisky with ginger beer and chloral hydrate, ads
that sing the ecstasy of an ample disposable income.

The Sick Muse

What's up, pussy-cat, got your period?
You've been staring at the screen for so long
that a hundred crime shows revolve and repeat,
mutating and blabbering at the back of your brain.
Have the girls who lurk around the perfume counters
of Macy's and Bloomingdale's like painted remoras
concocted for you the Essence of Nightmare,
and plunged you into a spa bath of Oblivion?
I prefer you tanned and sweating from a bike ride,
turning over in your mind a few of Wittgenstein's
more luminous aphorisms, while rehearsing
the gentle undulations of the exchange rate
to the tune of that enduring song, the hypnotic hymn
to the great Mammon, God of the Golden Dollar.

My Former Life

Longtemps, je me suis couché de bonne heure... – Proust

For a while there I used to go to bed
early, and sleep like a dormouse,
dreaming of honky-tonk saloons
and flying through a high, twilight sky.
At the beach, a red riot of holidays –
five miles of empty white sand
and behind a horizon of burning blue:
exotic palaces and heaps of creamy cloud.
My aunt and uncle brought me lemonade
and taught me obscure games. I caught fish
and cooked them for breakfast, and read stories
that seemed far-off and far-fetched. Let me
quickly grow older and stronger, I wished,
but don't lead me through the door of death.

Big Girl's Blouse

In the good old days mutations appeared everywhere,
and every second baby was a monster.
I wish I could have lived then, neighbour
to a gigantic young woman, like her pet hamster.
Her body would grow a foot a day, her legs
swell like tree trunks, and her childish play would
lay waste to housing estates. As adolescence
flushed her limbs, I would look for the first stirrings
of sexual desire. I would explore her body, crawling
around her nipples like an exhausted pilgrim
circumambulating a shrine, and when summer's
heat felled her vast bulk on the beach, I'd doze
inside her blouse between her breasts like a kitten
or James Stewart's invisible rabbit in *Harvey*.

Gypsies

Late last night, a crowd of young people
milled around the nightclub door, smoking,
chattering, adjusting their clothes, then
spilled out into the neighbouring streets
and alleys, the girls arm in arm, sharing
obscure and youthful secrets, young men
laughing at some crude joke,
testing and nudging each other.

The constellations crank forward
a little, night moves on, clouds hurry by,
as they disperse among the shadows of the buildings
that remind you of the endless blocks of flats
in Singapore, or the mise en scène for *Alphaville:*
silent skyscrapers, foggy street lights,
someone reading a book of poetry.

Dawn finds them slowly coming together
again, on the edge of the suburbs where
the roads grow narrower and less interesting,
and funnel into one highway, a thrash of traffic,
leading out into the countryside: that
astonishing tract of weeds and polluted creek-beds,
riverbanks strewn with paper and plastic waste,
scrub and scratchy branches, and no animals.
Over the hills they find a farm or two
deep in bone-breaking debt, a quarry
where a truck half full of gravel
rusts by a pool of water. A rabbit
watches them pass from his burrow,
crows look down on them hungrily,
a pale moon rides the distant ridge,
and night, once more, begins to darken the land.

Literature

I am the product of a million ambitions worked
into complex patterns of ink on paper or parchment.
My voice – classical, serene – calls to the young
and imprints the idea of perfection on their fevers.
Deep in the library stacks I contemplate rhetorical
strategies more ornate than a perfect game of chess.
No emotions permitted; unless properly blanched,
dressed and laid out in matching pairs, like gloves.
Writers, bowed down before those incomprehensible
centuries – before my vast cathedrals, noble careers,
processions of saints and emperors – will read and write,
absorb and excrete: bubbles afloat on the ocean
that mirrors the sky, blue under the brilliant
sun, glittering with fiery diamonds at night.

The Ideal

It will never be the models in the colour supplements –
those begging letters of a greedy age –
their lips giblets of silicone, their corrugated ribs,
who can inspire me with a flicker of lust.
I leave to Leibovitz, Laureate of Disney Parks,
her gallery of vanities, her circus of bloated egos,
for among those lipstick celebrities I cannot see
a single flower worthy of a vase.
The real need of my heart, deeper than a gutter,
is you, Lady Thatcher, soul annealed by politics,
or Nancy Reagan, born in the land of lies;
or Kylie the Idol, creature of Jeff Koons –
Kylie, pinned and wriggling in a magazine,
grinning like an inflatable doll in ecstasy!

Aphrodisiac

Calling to see you is like visiting a cemetery:
silence, wind in the grass, withered flowers.
Flask of vinegar, bitter cynic, you have
a sneer for every fashion, and an insult
for each of your friends. No one's good enough;
you even put me down, but that's fine;
I can handle worse shit than that. Where
do you get that high and mighty confidence?
You're hardly a star or a model of beauty,
and you're not so hot in bed. But lust
drives me to make a pass, to feast on your
bony body like a maggot on a carcass.
There's something about you naked on the carpet:
your cold disdain is a bracing aphrodisiac.

Perfume

My eyes closed, dozing on a summer afternoon,
I inhale the perfume you're wearing, wearing
nothing else: I see black volcanic sand,
waves flogging the shore, a harsh sun,
a country colonised by waves of capital
where every man conquers every other,
and the women run the joint, roaming at night,
seeking a casual coupling in the dark.
Spellbound by your perfume – *Eau d'Ivresse?* –
I see a hotel parking lot filled with Cadillacs,
the lobby crowded with realtors and call girls,
while the shrieks of peacocks roosting on the roof
echo through the crowded streets and mingle
with the hysterical laughter of the party-goers.

Pride

In the Age of Plastic, when Theory flourished
and young people read intellectual books,
one day a Californian Marxist Theoretician,
flushed with a tenure-track appointment
– after dazzling his competitors with arabesques
of paradoxes and non sequiturs, spiralling
metaphors that disappeared into their own
black holes, having astonished student
and professor alike, after flashing across
the smoky skies of academia, far above
the steaming pits of politico-linguistic theory
and the gauntlets of appointment committees –
which only French Academicians, perhaps,
had the proper savoir faire to navigate –
panic-stricken, like an acid freak on a bad trip,
like a nightclubber overdosed on Ecstasy,

he woke from a bad dream choked with simulacra
and cried out: 'Theory! I nurtured and raised you!
But had I wished to trip you up through
the defect of your initial faulty premise –
cultural formations are "like languages", they
have a "grammar" – why not "like roles", they
interact with other "roles" constituting
a "narrative" of social interaction? – why not
"like a circuit", interacting choices which
summed in Boolean groups constitute
a variable and cybernetic current of meaning? –
faulty, plausible simile – from which everything else
extends like a cantilevered road to nowhere –

your sudden fall from fashion and power
would far surpass the velocity of your takeoff,
and you would plunge to earth, a moral lapse,
a fashion blunder, a shameful memory, a fad!'

#

The thought was too much, and his brain snapped:
the eyes, once feverishly bright, now dimmed,
and clotted conspiracies clouded his horizon.
His mind, once as active as a switchboard,
as rich and as complex as a hologram,
fell silent like an abandoned repair shop
where car bodies rust, and spiders dream.

Now, among the lunch-hour crowds you'll find him
shambling aimlessly along, bearded, barefoot,
dirty, dazed by the simple sunlight,
inspecting a garbage bin with the eager care
he once devoted to a new hypothesis, a warning
to the ambitious executives who push past him
on their way to the cold grave that awaits us all.

The Mask

*An Allegorical Articulated Statue in the Style of
the Postmodern*

Get this: a giant toy escaped from Disneyland
to scamper clumsily and chortle in the fields of fashion,
guzzling bubbly, snorting coke, a perfect marriage
of gracefulness and mendacity. This thing –
female, perhaps, but not quite woman, slender
to an almost skeletal degree – you were invented
to cast your magic over a bank lobby, and
to charm those few and precious leisure hours
of a currency trader en route to somewhere else.

And get that smile: jerky, perhaps – but
who's perfect? – simulating the moment where
self-conceit becomes self-awareness through
the magic of computerisation, and displays its euphoria;
that sly, tardive grin, designed to be mocking,
attempting to appear languorous, the rubber lips
stretching and then swelling like a muffin:
that cute face, half doll, half prostitute,
framed in a veil of artificial human hair,
whose every feature speaks of the lab
that cobbled it together, saying 'Manga
made me, and the pleasures of children
ensure my financial viability!' Knockout!
To that assemblage of flexible joints and solenoids,
how the latex surface treatment adds
the final touch! But look at that thing at the top –

let's call it a head – it doesn't seem quite right,
and that slight cognitive dissonance is a turn-off.

Of course it's a mask, mobile, nearly human,
the lips smiling, then, with a faint grinding noise,
imitating a dainty scowl and opening wide
then closing like a goldfish – but inside the head,
through those eyes, those pupils like pulsing

lakes of laser light, something's going on
that seems the binary opposite of the emotions
presented by the superficial structural effects.
Poor half-creature! your sincere fakery
is constantly monitored and adjusted cybernetically,
to what avail? Your apparent wish to live is only
a calculated gesture; but where wishes come from –
the fear of death, the love of life, the urge to mate –
lies beyond the boundary of the simulacrum and the real.

Hair

Your hair, alternately spiky and flowing,
black and gold, with a lazy perfume,
you fill the hazy sky tonight with memories
of broken sleep and drifting hopes.
I run my fingers through it.

Some fill their ears with cool jazz;
I tousle your hair and dream: the drinks
and drugs of the sixties, London, brash
Singapore, the girly men of Bugis Street,
they live out their ghostly afterlife.

I'll go back there where shopping was a thrill,
where taxi-drivers and food-stall cooks
are driven crazy by the tourist dollar:
your perfumed hair holds a magic world
of jet engines and the scent of aviation fuel,

a shopping centre chill with air conditioning,
echoing with bouncy music, where the stores
are full of the latest electronic gadgets,
imitation Rolex watches for half price
and suits made up to fit in half an hour.

I've been working too hard lately,
and I need a break: I'll nuzzle your neck
and run my fingers through your hair,
and find myself taken away to the tropics
where a siesta is a well-earned reward

and no one gets up before midday.
The shops open then, but the bar
never closes, and from that peaceful twilight
you can hear waves lapping on the harbour-front
and the cries of hawkers on the street.

The scent of coconut oil and vanilla
mingles with exhaust fumes and those
clove-flavoured Indonesian cigarettes –
long ago, when we used to smoke and drink
and watch the dawn flood the tropic sky.

Hymn to Beauty

Did you step off the plane from L.A., or rise from the pit,
gorgeous? You look around, surprised to be alive,
kissing some, and pissing on the less fortunate.
You're like kif: some love it, some freak out.

Your bloodshot eyes glitter and shine: sunrise
and sunset; your perfume suffocates, your kisses
are their own poisonous aphrodisiac, paralysing
weight-lifters and giving old men erections.
Do you come from a fashion parade, or the sewer?
Journalists follow you around, noting
the dreams and the nightmares you scatter
about you, all party time and no responsibility.

You clamber over a heap of bodies you laugh at:
'What's up, sweetie? Nod off again?' Your necklace
of skulls spells out horror, and murder
takes you for a spin on the dance floor.
The dazzled window-dresser is drawn to you,
and makeup artists, perfumiers, young men
fond of old screen idols, kissing themselves
in the lipstick-smeared mirror of their desire.

Whether you're an angel or a slut, who cares,
or what sour chemicals infect your blood,
as long as your eager fingers in my pants
promise to arouse me to a novel bliss,
a cocaine country where the skies ripple
and flicker with enticing mirages, where
beautiful illusions fill the afternoons
with the promise of eternal happiness.

You Would Fuck Everybody

You would fuck everybody, and then
come back for more: slut! Boredom
makes you cruel and fuels your lust.
A handful of victims aren't enough: you need
a fresh conquest every day. Your eyes
like shop windows glittering with jewels
or laser cannon on a cruising gunship
scan the meat market and fasten on a target
using a borrowed source of energy
like a hooker with a hit of speed.

Sex machine, you give birth not to babies
but to new forms of emotional torture.
Men who fuck you deserve what they get,
is that it? As for shame, forget it, except for
the frisson of fear as you glance in a mirror:
how long do you have before it's all over,
how soon before those handsome boys
cross the street to avoid your grasping claws?
And then what? The bottle, or the grave?

But then, you might find a would be writer –
young, not too bright, in love with bullshit –
willing to wreck his sanity between your legs:
then you could boast, in your dotage, of how –
with a little sex, a little torment –
you fashioned a famous poet. You wish.

Hulk

Bad girl, dear creature, do you remember that thing
we saw one summer morning, wandering the paths
by Maggie's Farm: the carcass of a '39 Chev,
an oil-stained wreck in a tangle of weeds:
the headlights two scoops of glittery pebbles,
the radiator stained with a dribble of rusty water,
the engine block furred with grease and dust
and the steering wheel broken. The rust
and the rotting rubber and the chemicals
leaking from sump and battery gave back
to the soil various acids and heavy metals
that the generous earth had given,
in an elemental form, to factories
in China and Taiwan, liquids now escaped
from their silent, sealed utility and translated
to a cautiously-spreading poison.

Mantling a pool of fuming ruby liquid
a scum of brilliant green and scarlet
trembled and stared back at the sky.
There was a vague stink of oil and gasoline.
The sun looked down on that ruined thing,
burning the dented metal and blistered paint
that had been burned a thousand times before.

The angle of fender and running-board echoed –
so it seemed – a quickly-sketched motif
in a Francis Bacon painting I had seen in London;
the pattern of paint blotches and scratches of rust
on the bent flank reminded me of Mark Tobey

at his most subtle. Here, these graphic images
were only graphics because I looked at them,
just as, years ago, a crack in a particular footpath
had sketched a perfect design meant for nobody,
but one stared at and stored away by me.

#

But this decay and desolation waits for us all:
you too, when your time comes,
and the coffin is shovelled over with dirt
and the eternal darkness begins, when the worms
come to keep you company and strip you
to the bones, you too will be forgotten
decade after decade, century upon century,
forgotten among millions: but for this
brief reminiscence: a sketch that will fade,
but less quickly, while the language lives.

Paradise

Have pity on me, slumped on the floor
of the gambling palace, the carpet soaked.
Nothing much to see here except
Koreans and Chinese throwing money away.
All night long, bullshit blaring from the screens.
As many prawns as you can eat, for ten bucks:
I should have known better. A fluoro tube
flickers in the Men's – I hope this is the Men's.
It's horrible, the way the lights are always on,
like a police beating without the beating,
and the addicts with their ugly dreams,
crawling home at dawn, broke, ashamed,
falling into bed while the wife screams at them,
their only win: sleep, a kind of paradise.

Greed

Glib bimbo, brown as lukewarm porter,
scented with ketosis and smoker's breath,
work of some freak fashion designer,
Mephisto of the catwalk, fashionable goth:
compared to board meetings, to group travel,
I prefer sex with you on the Astroturf, and
when we play among the gloomy furniture,
your eyes are beer taps with neon handles.
Through those fountains beaded with a chill dew
you decant a brisk drink with a trace of bitters
and a dash of methedrine to wake me up,
a cocktail you might take before going to a movie:
Dark Passage, perhaps, with its implausible coincidences
and the lovely architecture of forties San Francisco.

Silk

Her dress is something else: silk
with a purple-green metallic sheen
that wavers and flows like a flag when she walks
downtown, past the crowded shop windows
where a second edition of herself echoes
her lazy perambulations, always
pausing when she pauses, looking away
when she bothers to look at the traffic.
Her eyes are pools of cloudy quartz,
and her stoned stare has the innocence
of a disoriented angel, unused to our ways,
but also something ancient and coldly knowing:
visitor from a planet of glass and steel, where
adults live forever, and there are no children.

The Serpent

Wild thing, how I love to see your skin
tanned to a deep caramel, as you doze
on the thick white rug, and your spiky hair
with its scent of drying beer shampoo,
that swirling sea with waves of orange and blue.

Like a rocket that wakes up with a rocket
up its arse my dopey soul shoots up, aiming
for the sky over Honolulu. Your eyes,
two blank screens where little is happening,
just dreamlets of gin and tonic, or sweeter
cocktails, are two cold jewels – citrine, say –
where tungsten and iridium cohabit.

You meander carefully down to the waterfront
in nothing much but underwear, abandoned
to the early winter sun and the scent of coffee,
the old men looking up from their papers.
Under your lowering hangover, your child-like head
sways and jerks to and fro, taking in the scene:
the trash, the snoring drunks, and God staring
at the wreck his mighty Creation led to.

Your body props like a ferry hitting the wharf
and recoiling in a wash of green foam
as you negotiate your morning Calvary.
Like a stream in spate from some passing storm,
when you gargle with a crystal mélange of vodka and fizz
then fasten those lips on mine it seems I'm drinking
Ecstasy and Bitters, a liquid sky
that scatters Pop-Rocks in my brain.

Vampire

You who punctured my heart
like a catheter dripping cyanide,
you who, strong as a Turkish
wrestler, bullied your way

into my apartment, my life,
my fizzing humiliated brain,
bitch I'm tied to like a mortgagee
chained to his extravagant loan,

punter to a string of losing horses,
speed freak to his handful of crystals,
fatty to his lard sandwiches,
arsehole, may you rot in hell.

I asked the great god Nembutal
to grant me endless sleep,
I took a bus to nowhere, I fled
to Surfers Paradise: you were there.

Drugs and travel both spoke to me
in a dream: the more you struggle
the deeper you sink – quicksand
is a merciful death compared to

what she has in store – the moment
you tore yourself away you would
run back to her, grovelling: rabbit
to the trap, pig to the slaughter.

One Night

One night I lay with a frightful Aryan,
like a Hitler Youth beside his Führer
except instead of dark-haired, sweaty and diseased
this blond hero was like an advertisement
for cotton singlets and after-shave lotion,
and lost in that spinning dark I began to calculate
the odds of surviving the destruction of the Reich,
then I thought of the 1933 election in Berlin
and the following 'enabling act' which spelled out
the death of democracy, and the whole nation
woke up in the grip of a nightmare that was
just beginning: first the breath of spring,
the clean streets and the glittering shards
of crystal, later the one hundred million deaths.

Remorse

When you sleep at last, my darling,
for the last time, beneath a slab of stone,
when the weight of that slab presses down
and crushes the breath from your breathless chest,
when your bedroom is a hollow box
six feet deep in the damp soil, when
you long for a flicker of light to illuminate
that horrid cave, thick with eternal dark,
your grave, like a sheriff in a black and white
Western, my confidante, for sheriffs are always
ready to listen to a poet, will sneer, and mock
in whisky-soaked tones: 'What's up, darling?
Couldn't you guess why the dead weep? Remorse
for a wasted life. Now say good night.'

Ghost Who Walks

1   THE DARKNESS

I'm almost used to the lack of light, the twilight
of murderous depression, sans drugs, where
nature and nurture have ensconced me,
    snarling and wriggling;

I'm like one of those old-fashioned
Futurists, painting black on black, or a
cannibal who cuts off his cock and eats
    casseroled penis;

but now and then when the weather's fine
a ghost stands in the glare of the doorway:
you have a visitor, sir: it's her, jewel,
    light of my nightmare,

mood-lifter, golden fit, angel,
ambassador from the world of industry,
from that innocent planet of light: her,
    dark, and yet glowing.

2   PERFUME

Remember: when you smell a flower,
or when you sip your Crème de Menthe,
or when you open an old book, the scent of
    black ink and resin?

A kind of magic takes you back decades,
and that lost kingdom, the past, lives
again, and makes you drunk; like that, your
    lover's new perfume

seems to thicken the air, weaving
in and out of her blonde hair: some
wild and savage scent, mingled
    orchid and tiger.

3 THE FRAME

The painting's dull, it's true – even though it's
by a modern master, today's Boucher –
muddled in its intentions, and the way that
    figure is looming

through the fog, hunched and bulky, unfortunately
suggests a gorilla on a lead – yet the frame –
selected by his dealer – pastel blue froth
    frozen and varnished

with pale gold – adds a lovely strangeness
to the whole ensemble. Thus her rope
of iridescent pearls, the emerald ring, the
    bangles and earrings

suited her weird looks to perfection;
the way that parrots, foliage and scarlet
flowers make a perfect background for a
    queen of the jungle,

on her awkward body that tangle
of jewellery was just right. She deserved it,
she said, when, under the spell of several
    Singapore Slings she

murmured and kissed me, her naked body quite
at home in satin and creamy linen, her limbs
moving with a kitten's childish grace,
    impish and cheeky.

4 The Portrait

Cruel time, that turns our budding passion
into a narrative, that engineers the sunset
and sees the moon rise, turns our youth to
　　ashes and cinders.

The quick glance, tender and mischievous,
your lips, the kisses soft as perfume,
the obsessions that lasted for days,
　　nothing is lasting.

But time, that gives birth to us, that kills
our love and wrecks us on the rocks
of age, can never destroy my
　　memory of you.

Little Dog

There you are, your paws on my knees,
your head tilted to one side. You gaze at me
with that puzzled look, your eyes full of
loyalty and complicated queries.
That cat I chased yesterday, where is it?
Who is that stranger? What's that scent?
Can we go for a walk now, and explore
 the paths that wind through the park by the bay?
Wise creature, you know where that bone
is buried, where the rats hide in their burrow
by the water, why the cat fears you.
You know many subtle facts, old friend,
except for one sad particular: how
brief a time we have left together.

The Duel

Two writers savaged each other: reviews,
Letters to the Editor, then a brawl at a gallery
with broken glass and shrieking socialites –
youth, drink, vanity, sexual rivalry.
Soon it's teeth and claws and pulling hair,
curses, a skull thudding on the floor, more
broken glass, insults: 'Brown-nosing your way
into the colour supplements! Fraud! Failure!'
In the back alley haunted by thugs and junkies
our heroes rolled against a garbage bin,
punching, the air full of grunts and shouts:
this alley is the hell of writers, crowded with
ourselves. Fight, gossip; go on: write it up,
so our sordid quarrels will become immortal.

A Present

Hey, sweetheart, here's a poem, take it
or leave it. One day, in the mysterious future,
these lines blown roughly off-course
may come to rest in a library, to amuse
a bored reader for a while. My portrait of you
will float above the limping syllables
and by the special magic of art, drift
in the haze of imagination, above the page.
Why do I bother? It's hardly your charm, from
Paris to Peoria no one likes you much;
those who know you give you a wide berth.
You mock the talented and sneer at the stupid
as though God had set you up in judgment;
more demon than angel, but utterly lovely.

Devil

The sun was hidden in a red cloud. Be like that;
don't answer the phone, cover your face,
sleep – or, half asleep, watch the ads on TV,
wander in the kitchen, bore yourself to death,
I love you like that! But if you wish,
slip out of your sheath like a rapier, wander
downstairs and get a hit of something
at Tony's and cruise the Strip, drift among
the loonies and the damaged, cruise the crowd
and flirt with the sex tourists in the glare
of shop windows. To me you're hot to go,
pissed off or pouting, glazed or galvanised,
done up in furs or naked on all fours,
whatever: Devil of Death, you're adorable.

Ever the Same

'Why the long face?' you asked. Okay,
you're talking to a depressive, does that
give you a clue? And I forgot my tablets.
And life is a bowl of horse shit.
There's nothing philosophical about it:
Blind Freddie could tell you that.
So save your breath. You're sweet, great
tits, gorgeous body, but you're no Einstein.
And why the cheery disposition, darling?
Don't you know that we all have to die?
You call that fair? It's horrible – but your eyes,
so clear and beautiful: I'd like to sink into them,
and sleep – of course it's an illusion – sleep
like the stupid, happy child I used to be.

Grey Sky

With your gaze like train tracks disappearing
    at the horizon, eyes tiny screens with
nothing on but that buzzing, dancing snow, you
    remind me of months spent in a hospital:

fields of pale fog, the scent of disinfectant,
    nerves plucking and jabbing at my sleep.
Sometimes you're a car crash: five vehicles
    in a pile-up, lights flashing; or a factory set alight,

where fire hoses gush and spurt all night long.
    Dangerous bitch! When you're pissed off, look out:
the shriek of tyres on an icy road, clanging steel,
    pleasures sharper than a hypodermic.

After Midnight

What will you say tonight, after the TV news
is over and done, after the midnight movie:
The Conversation, let's say, with the murderous
twist at the end, and that lonely jazz –
after a stroll on the terrace to watch the stars
glitter overhead, what will you say to her
whose glance at a crowded gallery opening
revived you, encouraged you to hope, again...
you could say that she's cute, and sexy,
but that's predictable and opportunistic;
that it is an honour to do her a favour, that
her slightest glance is like lightning, that
you are alive only because of her, and other
such compliments and flattering remarks.

Screen Angels

I see them in the air, creatures of the screen,
born of stories concocted for money to feed
the crowd with a perfectly average IQ.
Makeup, lighting and action have rendered them
magnetic, and they shine in front of the cameras,
quite at home in bizarre landscapes and those
almost unbelievable narratives – our stories,
if we were only spies, heroes or gamblers.
They die every time 'The End' appears floating
over their foreheads, but they live again
and again, and a thousand deaths fail
to extinguish their eerie flame. Like the legendary
kings and queens and heroes and monsters of old
they fill the night skies with winking stars.

All of Her

The Devil dropped by today,
just to test me, to try and find a fault,
as he always does. 'Tell me, what is it,'
he asked, 'about that dumb bitch

that turns you on? I don't get it.'
Give me a break! 'Oh, her breasts,'
I said, 'haven't you noticed those
tender buds, peeping through her dress?'

But I was kidding: the whole ensemble,
that's what does it: not the hair, though
the hair is a riot of gold and burgundy,
not the eyes, like crystal lakes, the skin

smooth and perfect, the lips like rosebuds,
blah, blah, the simple bodily facts
the Prince of Darkness here would easily get.
It's something else, made up of all these:

she shines like the sun coming up,
she soothes like gentle nightfall, but
it's the harmony bchind all this
that makes her perfect.

Evening Harmony

Late Summer, Autumn, seasons made for verse:
    flowers reek like perfume in a bowl.
Dentists' wives and call girls take a stroll;
    songs that moan and echo like a curse.

Flowers reek like perfume in a bowl.
    Country and western, steel guitars, and worse,
songs that moan and echo like a curse.
    The sky is blue, like fifties rock and roll.

Country and western, steel guitars, and worse:
    A heart of metal, and a plastic soul.
The sky is blue, like fifties rock and roll.
    The clouds that choke the sun are like a hearse.

A heart of metal, and a plastic soul.
    You are sweeter than a sexy nurse.
The clouds that choke the sun are like a hearse.
    Your memory flutters like a burning coal.

Poison

Wine: drink enough, and your miserable room
seems quite habitable, in fact almost luxurious:
the sunset flares among the clouds
only to illuminate your immense talent,
and the moonlight brings oblivion.

Opium takes you somewhere else entirely:
Luna Parks of glowing marble, brilliant
philosophies that travel rapidly beyond
the blue horizon, everlasting life, your doubts
dissolved, your wishes fulfilled.

The poison that leaks and glows from
your bloodshot green eyes, those mirrors
that show me my grimacing spirit at its worst...
my chattering dreams wheel, flock and settle
there, to sip that sour draught.

But your kisses: wet tongue and lipstick
that tastes of sugar and cheap perfume,
your acid saliva tainted with lunacy and paranoia,
lust that plunges my shaking soul into
a pit of darkness by the shores of death.

The List

Here's an idea: I make a list and write it down:
your various good points, your voice, your beauty,
youthful skin, knees, ankles, chin, bodily and
spiritual charms, and so forth: awesome princess!

A better idea: write the list in violet ink,
soak it in alcohol, wrap it in cotton wool,
send it to a non-existent person Poste Restante
in some tropical country, far into the future.

So: when you frock up and head out the door
you're like a Boeing 747 as it starts down the runway,
engines slowly rising to a thunder, freighted
with tourists and executives and their woozy dreams.

In the store, you stare at the milling customers
as though they had no right to be there,
shopping with you in this Palace of Luxury,
half stoned, and nicely soothed by tablets.

Your breasts, that startle the passing crowd,
they swell the spangled front of your new outfit;
they're like a parliamentary double dissolution,
or a pair of songwriters, Lieber and Stoller, say,

who penned *Hound Dog*, or a double
strawberry sundae with pink cherries on top.
Your chest a liquor cabinet full of sweet
concoctions; your legs, and what's between them...

When you dress up and hit the town
you're like a combine harvester assaulting
a field of ripe wheat, whirling, thrashing,
flinging admirers aside and surging forward,

your legs beneath your swaying dress outdo
the twin cylinders of a Harley-Davidson,
like two passionate lesbians who cross and
criss-cross in the frenzy of the tango.

Your arms rival those huge electro-magnets
that gather up tons of crushed vehicles
and dash them to earth with a crash of metal:
deal thus! with your tiresome lovers!

And when the taxi brings you home at dawn,
that ravishing, vivacious machine slows down:
a generous nightcap, and you sink like a submarine
deep into the night-blue cathedrals of sleep.

Grab Your Passport

Hey, significant other,
let's head off
overseas, somewhere
tropical: drugs all day,
sex all night,
floating in a landscape
that looks like you:
what a blast!

The watery sunlight
fondles the palm trees,
the skies are half blue,
half cloudy, or misty,
like your eyes:
treacherous,
tearful, smiling.

It has the charm
of a five-star hotel: luxurious-
looking, nicely decorated,
lots of servants, nothing to do
and all day to do it in.

Great lobby: mottled mirrors,
old furniture smelling of beeswax
like you see in *Vogue* magazine,
maids everywhere
chattering to each other –
gossip about the guests –
in that funny lingo they have.

Luxurious-looking, nicely decorated,
lots of servants, nothing to do
and all day to do it in.

#

Down by the waterfront
tankers, yachts, barges,
boats full of bananas
rocking on the current:
they're here for you,
honey-bun: have a banana.

And when the sun sinks
and lights up the sky with flame
somewhere over Sumatra,
the whole city glows
with reflected gold: like us,
snoozing in the twilight.

Luxurious-looking, nicely decorated,
lots of servants, nothing to do
and all day to do it in.

The Creature

Somewhere at the back of my mind
a creature strolls about, enjoying
the scenery: a seaside holiday and an old
novel in French, which I can't read.

When I was a child I longed for
an invisible friend, like the other kids
said they had. Shaving, I notice him
gazing back at me: here he is.

See how he conducts the orchestra
of sleepyheads, wordlessly.
Now and then he sings to himself
in a resonant baritone: some song

about predicting the rise and fall
of the market – his grand obsession.
His voice sounds like that of a distant
newsreader, it soaks into the depths

of my brain, and seems to be speaking
in rhyming verse in Middle English;
it affects me like gin and phenobarbital,
bringing ecstasy like a blow to the head.

Wow, there's no drug like this, its
mechanism so elegant: floating above
the Côte d'Azur on a Monday morning,
drunk and vigorous, eating an egg.

A Talk

You'd think the autumn sky would cheer me up:
across the horizon, pale veils of purple and rose.
But sadness rises up like gastric reflux,
and the whole cinematic effect is ruined.
Take your hand out of my pants, it's no use:
I'm used up, wrung out, hungry women have
teased and tormented me, devoured what's left
of my soul and wrecked my sex drive.
My heart is like a public toilet in a park at night:
gangs of drunks drink there, and try to fuck –
ah, your breasts are gorgeous, soft, perfumed...
you might want it, but you can't have it!
Burn me up with the raging flames in your eyes,
and take the shreds they left me with.

Obsession

Shopping malls, you terrify me like a noisy morgue,
your constant movement is like peristalsis
where millions of creatures are born and die
and are immediately reborn again, shopping.
And sports arenas: horrible! Filled with massed
attentive crowds, who do nothing but watch
and, at a climax, shriek and roar in unison
like a thousand mindless beasts driven mad.
The night sky would be much more pleasant
without those stars: I know their language, and
much prefer the silent void between them,
a vast movie screen where old friends
come to life, briefly, and smile at me,
friends long gone into their early graves.

Afternoon Song

Though your strange glance and your
slightly misshapen face give you
an odd look, not quite angel, more
    wicked magician,

I think you're adorably paranormal,
and I worship you with the dogged
reverence of those idiots who
    worship the devil.

Where did you get that shampoo?
Your hair smells of the forest,
and as your profile turns it's by turns
    fey and cartoonish.

That perfume you bought at Duty Free
is a wraith in praise of artifice;
you charm the guys in the band,
    also the cleaners.

Your laziness has more energy
than a hydroelectric turbine, and
your lewd caresses would give a
    corpse an erection!

When you need to flush your
system, a sex fit is just right,
you rip me open, and,
    lavish with kisses,

tear out my heart and
trample on it, laughing
like a psycho – why do I
   let you torment me?

why have I spent all my talent
making you happy, heat-seeking
rocket whose phosphorus
   warhead ignites me?

Goats and Monkeys

Top executives and poets alike, when they
grow old, keep pets: marmosets, little horses
with ribbons around their necks, capybaras,
cats, dogs, pigs, goats and monkeys.
They fight and make a mess in the attic and
fool around with the computer when he's out,
and if he asks a young woman to join him
at supper, they rush out and frighten her to death.
Happy creatures! When they dream, they snore,
and their chorus of murmurs lulls him to sleep.
The smell of their shit is everywhere, and
through the night he suffers horrid nightmares:
cleaning the Augean Stables with his tongue;
flinging handfuls of dung at his ex-wife.

Drunks

Under the trees in the dusty park
drunks gather in the evening
like a flock of moth-eaten owls,
glancing about, red-eyed, obsessive.
They'll sag and rest there, motionless,
sipping from a bottle in a paper bag
until the street lights flicker into life
and dusk falls on the heartless city.
They're hardly philosophers, or Buddhist saints,
but they have many things to teach us,
should we watch and listen: keep quiet,
keep to yourself, and don't be noticed.
Look at those commuters in the early sun:
hearts pounding, rushing to an early grave.

Spleen

Too many memories! An old mainframe,
choked with a hopeless tangle of COBOL code,
databases with a hundred million fields – debts,
names, addresses, medical conditions –
has fewer files than the back of my brain.

I am a small-town library, forgotten for years,
stuffed with old papers and unread novels;
a sales yard with heaps of out-of-date cars
waiting, as the traffic roars past, for
some potential sucker to pull up
and kick a few tyres. I am a second-hand shop
with smelly old dresses hanging on a rack,
a heap of paperback airline novels
long out of fashion, a print of dogs
playing billiards, and chipped crockery.

Time seems to crawl, in my dismal apartment;
it takes an hour to make a cup of tea,
and I spend a whole afternoon looking through
that cardboard box full of old photos.
Boredom stretches and fills my days
like a zeppelin, or a lifetime's calling
you need a good degree to be admitted to.

I've turned into a statue, mounting
silent guard over a desert visited by
sand storms and endless fields of cloud,
forgotten, lost, not marked on any map,
a god whose ancient and eternal rage
sings only in the glow of the setting sun.

To a Creole Lady

I had some accumulated leave, so I took this
Seniors' Tropical Cruise, and in Creoletown
I met this lady by the road one evening,
under the street lights and shadowy trees.
What a stunner! She was selling hot curry,
or some such, and a drink like rum and chillies,
and I don't remember much more except
the moon spinning around, and the next day
I said 'Babe, if you came with me to Paris,
cruised the Left Bank, or the banks of the Seine,
the guys would be all over you! You'd make
a fortune – uh – selling that drink, and the poets –
I know dozens of poets – they would willingly
throw themselves at your feet. How about it?'

Country Music

Country music transports me like a sports car to my
    favourite barroom.
Under a ceiling of fog, thick with circling planes, I
    rev up the motor,
wheels squealing at the turns, my mouth panting
    like an old hound-dog's,
I roar along the expressway and through suburbs
    noisy with shopping.
Wheeling through my brain are all the accidents
that could happen, but don't, thanks to my
    debonair driving:
through the city I go and into the dark country, where –
distant, scattered – the occasional farmer sleeps, chilled,
    wrapped in his mortgage.

Seven Old Men

Swarming city, ant-hill by the harbour,
choked with office workers and strange dreams,
where ghosts live in the cellars under the street.

One evening – thick and filled with mist –
I was looking for a bar down by the waterfront
where the streets are less crowded, and garbage

blocks the gutters. I noticed an old man
dressed like an executive down on his luck,
his suit worn, his cuffs ragged. I swore

I recognised him from the evening news
some months ago: his business in collapse,
accusations of fraud staining his knighthood,

his offshore bank accounts the subject of scrutiny.
Once he'd rubbed shoulders with the Prime Minister,
they were often seen together on his private yacht;

now he limped, and I noticed a stick; his sour look
would strip paint from a wall, and suppressed emotions
mottled his unshaven face with rage.

His likeness shadowed him: another executive
once a famous name, now disgraced,
a kind of evil twin; the same shabby suit,

the same stubble, the same stare full of hate.
And then another one... seven of them,
limping, snarling, through the stinking dusk.

I walked quickly away, and found my bar,
and soon drowned my fears. But those
apparitions still haunt my sleep.

Landscape

High up on the library roof, the south wind's
voice whistling on the tiles and the faint
murmur of the city are the only sounds.
I look down at the ants busily hurrying
from home to work, from bed to factory,
rivers of vehicles choking the freeways,
and the skies over the fish markets
thick with golden cumulus.

As dusk creeps over the city the street lights
blink on, one by one, and the neon signs
take up the chorus, shouting their slogans,
then the lights of the buses, winding through
my favourite thoroughfares, where the shop windows
spill their glare onto the footpaths. Then the rising
moon floods the Pacific with glitter.

I see the good times come and go, the exchange rate
reflecting the fears and the greedy passions
of the investors, rising and falling, bank loans
more or less costly as the market fluctuates.
Winter robs the poplars of their golden harvest,
and I make my way down to the stacks, where
old forgotten books doze in the gloom.

There I painstakingly construct my palaces
and temples of memory. There the busy streets
of Kabul live again, as they were in sixty-seven;
Orchard Road is brash with hawkers and the scent
of frying spices: brawls, hallucinations,
ecstasies throng there.

Let those electrical storms
roll over the city; I'm happy
bent over the screen, fiddling with sapphics,
tuning and adjusting a recalcitrant adonic –
obstinate rhythm – as the wind throws
rain at the windows.

Afterword

THE 56 POEMS in the last part of this book were written during a six-week Fellowship at the Civitella Ranieri centre in Umbria, Italy, in 2009. I should like to thank David Lehman for putting my name forward, the trustees and board of the Civitella Ranieri Foundation for their generosity in granting this Fellowship, and the staff and fellow guests for making my stay so pleasant and productive.

With a French novelist in mind, I have titled this group of poems 'Contre-Baudelaire'. They began as radical revisions, updatings and reinterpretations of some poems from Charles Baudelaire's *Les Fleurs du mal.* I should add that in the poems that appear here, the apparent obsession with sex, drugs, betrayal, bodily decay, death and graveyards is mainly Baudelaire's, and that when its presence in various of his poems became too rich for my taste I left them by the wayside.

Many of the earlier poems in this book, often as a different version, formed part of my creative arts doctoral thesis at the University of Wollongong, which was written from 2005 to 2008. The first three poems explore, in different ways, the idea of displacing the authorial ego with a kind of writing at one or two removes, through the process of translation, ventriloquy, mask or disguise.

Some years ago I was asked by the Toronto magazine *The Modern Review* to write an essay on John Ashbery's long poem 'Clepsydra', published in the collection *Rivers and Mountains* in 1966. A number of other writers were also invited to do the same. I had already written on various aspects of John Ashbery's work, so instead, in 'The Anaglyph', I took the first word or two and also the last word or two of each line from John Ashbery's poem, and wrote material of my own to fill each line out. An *anaglyph* is a drawn or photographic image, usually printed in red and bluish-green ink, that, when viewed through spectacles containing one bluish-green lens and one red lens, presents a three-dimensional image; that is, an image consisting of two superimposed and differently-coloured views of the same scene.

'Desmond's Coupé' is a mainly homophonic translation (rather, mistranslation) of Stéphane Mallarmé's 1897 poem 'Un coup de dés...'

'Five Quartets' is a truncated version of T.S. Eliot's poem 'Four Quartets' which lacked Ezra Pound's severe editorial advice and which, at nearly 1,000 lines, seemed to me to be far too long. This version is Eliot's poem with most of the words removed, and runs to a more economical seventy-five lines.

The 83 poems from 'Hôtel de Ville' to 'Hair of the Dog' present deliberate mistranslations, involving multilingual dealings with an English-only speech-to-text computer program, of most of Rimbaud's 'Illuminations' and poems by Baudelaire, Mallarmé and Verlaine, dictated in my Australian-accented French. The poems have been reworked extensively, and each contains an added line or phrase from various poems by John Ashbery, though in a few cases these have been lost when the poems were revised. Several of these poems, mostly in a different form, appeared in my collection *Urban Myths* in 2006.

The group of eight poems in 'At the Movies' speak about various movies and their cultural settings: *The Forbidden Planet*, 1956 ('Caliban'); *Columbo* (crime television series), 1971–2003; *The Last Clean Shirt*, 1964 (by film maker Alfred Leslie and poet Frank O'Hara); *The Glass Bottom Boat* (also known as *The Spy in Lace Panties*), 1966; *Vertigo*, 1958 ('Boy in Mirror'); *Paris Blues*, 1961; and *Laura*, 1944 ('The Cedar Bar, NYC, 1957'). 'Rink' is based on a rejected scene from the hypothetical movie *Skater*, David Lynch, 1976.

THROUGHOUT THIS BOOK, where a stanza break occurs at the foot of a page, and where the stanza break might not be obvious because the poem is not set in regular stanzas, a hash (UK) or pound (US) symbol in the right margin indicates the stanza break, thus:

#

I SHOULD LIKE TO THANK the Literature Board of the Australia Council for its support during the writing and revising of this material, the Faculty of Creative Arts at the University of Wollongong and the Australian Government's Department of Education, Employment and Workplace Relations for an Australian Postgraduate Award that enabled a period of study in the Faculty of Creative Arts at the University of Wollongong, and my thesis supervisor John Hawke (then) at that university for his sensitive and insightful advice.

For many years Philip Mead has engaged with my poetry in an intelligent and helpful way: in particular his writing on cinema, psychoanalysis, and literary and cultural strategies has been of immense benefit to me in forming my critical thinking and poetic practice in the thesis part of this book, and elsewhere.

I OWE SPECIAL THANKS to Mr Ashbery for permitting me to eviscerate his poem 'Clepsydra' and to re-galvanise it as my poem 'The Anaglyph'.

None of this book could have been written without the background of my fifty-year career as a writer, and none of that would have been possible without the support and encouragement of my wife Lyn Tranter.

Index of First Lines

Made in the USA
Monee, IL
08 July 2026